P9-DBS-587

The Dynamics
of Liturgy

By H. A. Reinhold

The American Parish and the Roman Liturgy
Bringing the Mass to the People
The Soul Afire
The Dynamics of Liturgy

The Dynamics of Liturgy

H. A. REINHOLD

FOREWORD BY

RT. REV. MONSIGNOR EDWARD G. MURRAY

New York
The Macmillan Company
1961

nihil obstat: JACOB C. SHINAR, J.C.L.
             Censor Deputatus

imprimatur: ✠ JOHN WRIGHT
             Bishop of Pittsburgh

September 23, 1960

First Printing

The Macmillan Company, New York
Brett-Macmillan Ltd., Galt, Ontario

Printed in the United States of America

Library of Congress catalog card number: 60-12954

Foreword

It is a happy task to undertake a few words of prelude to this work, which, within the compass of its relatively few pages, gives a magisterial treatment to the questions raised by the renewed liturgical interest of our day. This book, which is so current in its interest, is made up of many essays written at various times over the past twenty years by Father Reinhold. The consistency of his approach to these matters gives evidence of the thoughtfulness and learning which he brings to them. There has grown up within the past five decades a sophistication within the ranks of our Catholic people which makes purely passive attitudes toward the liturgy inadequate for them, as the center of their spiritual lives. A generation which is challenged to the roots of its primary loyalties wishes to avoid even the appearance of formalism in its life of prayer. The centralities of our worship cluster about the Table and the Cross and these are brought together in the Altar where Christ's promises and the memory of His Passion constitute for all time the Action of Presence, Praise and Prayer.

It is noteworthy that whatever is presently offered with the appearance of newness is rather evocation of the earliest, of the primal Christian heritage. Christ, who washed the feet of His disciples, Christ who walked about the table to give Himself as food and drink, cannot be to the Christian of today a distant figure. What concerns His promised presence among us is in one way concealed always under the veil of mystery. This is the reason why in no other way must it be concealed, whether by rood-screen or apathy, or irrelevancies of whatever sort.

It is not in terms of mere love for the archaic or the mere retracing of development that there has been such a world-wide renaissance of interest in the liturgy during this century. It is in terms of nearer approach to Our Lord in the Sacrament of His Love for us and union with us that we seek something again of the nearness and friendship of the Pasch that He ate with His disciples. It is the Mass that matters and the meaningful union of all the faithful with their servant, God's priest at the altar, makes the Mass matter more to them. The liturgical revival of our time accepts the unchanging value of the Mass before the Throne of Grace, but seeks to make that value better understood by the congregation in the weakness of human language and analogy.

One of the sections of this book which will have a universal interest is the history of the dedicated scholarship which lies behind the modern revival of liturgical interest. It has been well said that things do not just happen, they are caused. Under Divine Providence, the learned priests, whose activities Father Reinhold limns for us, were the cause of renewed insight into the special qualities of the Latin Rite and by extension into the common riches of the variegated rites which express the same liturgical fact.

One day, when another generation makes its own inquiry into these questions, Father Reinhold will have his own place, and that not least, among the leaders of the liturgical revival. The very pages of this book are instinct with the erudition which Father Reinhold sets forth for our admiration in others. In special fashion we note those qualities which he undertakes to encourage in the many who turn to him for enlightenment and encouragement. He underlines the spareness, the austerity, which is the special genius of the Latin Rite. Conversely, he sheds light upon the ways in which sentimentality or well meant maladresse could lead us away from that stark understatement which is our liturgical heritage and the patrimony to be preserved in the Western Church.

In no way can we appreciate the Rites of the East adequately until we come to a historic and personal confrontation with our own Rite of the West. Its many riches are set forth for us in this book, which places us under added debt to its author. He has made the years of his illness fruitful by this enterprise, whereby we become sharers of his irenic and universal viewpoint. I share the hope of all his friends that this work may have that wide diffusion and influence which its qualities deserve.

EDWARD G. MURRAY, S.T.D.

Acknowledgments

I wish to thank all those who have helped me to prepare this book for its final form, and in particular the Most Reverend John J. Wright, Bishop of Pittsburgh, for his constant encouragement, Monsignor Edward G. Murray for his kind introduction, and Father Thomas J. Carroll who read the manuscript and made valuable suggestions.

To Dom Lambert Beauduin of Mont César and Chevetogne, a prophet in his own country and first articulate promoter of a better understanding of Pastoral Liturgy, this book is a token of gratitude and a small monument.

Contents

The Dynamics
of Liturgy

The Beginnings
of the Liturgical Movement

THE CLOISTER AND SOCIETY

On an afternoon in 1913 the abbot of Maria Laach, in the Eifel
Mountains near the Rhine, received four or five young men in one
of the parlors of the eight-hundred-year-old monastery. They had
asked for an interview because they wanted advice on their spiritual
lives. One of them was Paul Simon, another was Professor Hermann
Platz of Bonn University, a third was Father Kerkhey who later
became preacher at Münster Cathedral and confessor of the whole
city, and there was also young Dr. Heinrich Brüning.

Abbot Stotzingen with his customary friendliness asked them to
state their problems. He was not a little surprised when he heard
what these young laymen and future priests wanted from him. He
told them that he had a man in his monastery who might be able to
help them—a young and very learned monk by the name of Dom
Ildefonse Herwegen, who had often talked to him about his problems and who, strangely enough, as far as the abbot could remember,
had not only touched upon the same matters but had even used the
same terms.

So Dom Herwegen was called, and the young monk and these
men of the world found themselves in perfect agreement. Thus
began a revival that seized first the intelligentsia of Germany, then
spread to the young clergy, invaded parishes and organizations,
overcame the prejudices of religious superiors, and is now the consolation of millions.

The case was very simple, and it now seems incomprehensible that anyone could have looked on these endeavors as revolutionary. These men wanted nothing but their legitimate share in the liturgical life of the Church. They wanted to know what "it was all about." They felt the existence of a gap between their personal piety and the official worship on the altar that no one had been able to bridge. They had been sitting patiently through their Sunday Masses, saying their rosaries, singing popular hymns, or listening to the concert-like performance of a first- or second-rate choir. Some of them had even handled a missal in the vernacular—but they could not make head or tail of it even when they were initiated into such subtleties as the "ordo" and even when they did not fail to keep up with the priest.

What had all this to do with their personal happiness, their approach to Almighty God, their sanctification? Were these all dead formulas, relics of antiquity and the Middle Ages, jealously preserved by clerics who did not know themselves why they adhered to such petrified and circumstantial rites in our fast-living and subjectivist times? Or was there any meaning in this odd assortment of anthems, lessons, gospels, and prayers? Could they be used to deepen personal prayer? Could they be resuscitated by the individual and by a community, a community of men and women, children and old people, laborers and students who were not antiquarians and esthetes? Could all this become daily bread for the ordinary Catholic, or was it to be caviar for an élite? Must there continue always to be a clerical track for expresses to heaven while lay people rode slow trains freighted with popular devotions that had little in common with the things behind the altar rail but some general ideas and good intentions? Or was not the Church's prayer and sacrifice really the prayer and sacrifice of the whole Church, that is, all the faithful?

The outcome of this meeting was an invitation to these men and their friends to come back to Maria Laach for Holy Week, 1914. This was the first "Liturgical Week," which developed so amazingly into one of the permanent institutions of German Catholicism and bore such tremendous fruit.

World War I interrupted this new movement. But no sooner was it over than the first of a series of publications appeared. Romano Guardini opened the series, "Ecclesia Orans," with his now famous booklet *The Spirit of the Liturgy.*

For me, when I read this book, the restrictions and commandments that had seemed to be the essence of Catholicism, and that I had defended in fierce and dull despair, vanished before the vision of Christ's Mystical Body and the incredible beauty of His Mystical Life among us through His sacraments and mysteries. For thousands of my Catholic fellow countrymen this book opened a new approach to Catholicism and gave them a deeper understanding and love of our holy Faith. We could hardly wait for the following volumes of the "Ecclesia Orans," Dom Hammenstede's *Liturgy as Experience,* and Dom Casel's two revolutionizing little booklets on the Mass as "Mysterion" and the real meaning of the Holy Canon.

At the same time the best speakers of the abbey, including Abbot Herwegen, who had meanwhile succeeded Abbot Stotzingen, traveled over Germany and spoke to large and small audiences, inviting them to their monastery. They met the leaders of the Catholic youth and intelligentsia, and addressed priests in retreats and conferences. At the same time scientific series devoted to liturgical sources, liturgics, and historical research were initiated under the leadership of Abbot Herwegen, and the cooperation of the best German and foreign historians was enlisted.

The Liturgical Weeks were soon followed by retreats based on the liturgy and on a piety of definitely objective and sacramental character. This example was imitated by other abbeys and religious societies, and finally three great agencies accomplished what a small community of monks could not, a nation-wide popularization. These three agencies were the Akademikerverband, a national union of Catholic university graduates in all professions; the huge Catholic youth organizations with their millions of members; and the Popular Apostolate for Liturgical Revival at Klosterneuburg near Vienna. They embraced the ideas of Maria Laach with profound enthusiasm, and within about fifteen years piety and devotion had been relinked to the "official" worship of the Church and its sacramental and biblical character in a degree that may have been realized only in some golden age of liturgy.

There was a period at the beginning of this liturgical movement when everyone was in such high spirits, especially the young clergy and students, that those who, with however little justification, claimed to stand for sound "tradition" had need to warn against exaggeration. I remember times when young people, in their joy at discovering the superior evangelical beauty of the liturgical "world," wanted to abolish altogether such popular substitutes as the Stations and the Rosary. But this purist fervor was never very widespread and never deserved those bitter attacks launched against a "new heresy" by narrow and overanxious "guardians of the Faith."

In spite of my own enthusiasm for the Church's prayer, I was very skeptical when I arrived at Maria Laach in 1920. One of the novices showed me the crypt of the glorious old Romanesque abbey church and pointed out that the lay brothers and novices had their community Mass there every morning, at which they recited the Gloria and Credo in common with the celebrant, replied in unison to his acclamations, and took part in an Offertory procession, bringing their own altar bread to the altar rail—thus reviving a custom that died out only a few centuries ago and that is now replaced by the certainly more prosaic money collection at the Offertory.

Since I was on my way back from Rome, I was not shocked at the fact that the altar was facing the people, because I had seen this in all the major churches in Rome and I thought this was much more sensible than for the priests to turn their back to those with whom they were acting the *Sacrum Mysterium* of Our Lord's Sacrifice. I thought, however, that at the abbey they were too romantic, just "crazy about vestments and all the external paraphernalia"— an attitude I had acknowledged with an indulgent smile in certain high Anglican communities who built themselves cozy little monasteries in Italian Romanesque and established themselves like Sicilian *curati*.

But I had been rash. The next morning at Mass I discovered that this was really the form that enabled me as a layman truly to share in the Church's sacrifice. This form flowed quite naturally from the real meaning of the Mass; it was almost suggested by its ceremonies and texts. The amazing thing was only this—why on earth had it not been thought of before? The atmosphere was normal and manly, and the gray-bearded old lay brothers were just as happy and at home in "their" Mass as the fervent young students fresh from the universities.

Two little incidents show that things did not always go so smoothly as might have been expected. Wild rumors had been spread throughout Germany, especially among the clergy. These monks of Maria Laach had invented a new liturgy, had disregarded our good old (and comfortable) traditions, were advocating a lay priesthood that would destroy the respect for the priesthood proper and that almost smacked of Luther's doctrine of a universal priesthood.

One beautiful afternoon the seven mighty bells of our old minster rang, and a limousine drove up to the gates. In it was the Cardinal Archbishop of Cologne. Apparently "Headquarters" had asked him to look into the matter and to find out what sort of *Mysteria* the monks and their guests were performing. Well, the result of this visit was that next morning a certain member of the Sacred College had tears in his eyes and that a year or so later he stood behind a portable altar in his own huge cathedral saying the *missa recitata* with the whole congregation. And from then on, at all the annual Catholic congresses in Germany, with their ten thousands of faithful attending, the Nuncios have said the Mass facing the congregation, and very often reciting the appropriate prayers with all those present.

As a natural consequence of this return to Bible and liturgy, very soon the popular substitutes and the hitherto extraliturgical practices and devotions became more imbued with liturgical and biblical spirit, and much of the sentimental and pseudo-baroque trash of the late nineteenth century dropped out. Once familiar with the central mystery of the Church, the faithful soon demanded more of the true bread of Christ. Baptisms, which hitherto had appeared to be a legal performance in a corner of the church, with much mumbling, salt, and other strange practices, regained in its performance its old majestic beauty, and many dioceses gave as many texts as possible in the vernacular. This happened, *mutatis mutandis*, with Extreme Unction, Matrimony, and Holy Orders. People no longer liked fifteen-minute Masses, and rushing through other ceremonies. And the clergy were glad to see their flock participate in the most vital and essential things of Catholic life. The heart of the faithful in their religious life began to beat in rhythm with the Church, or, as Guardini has put it, the Church awoke in the souls of the faithful.

The hierarchy hesitated only a short time to acknowledge this popular movement inaugurated by monks. Of course, exaggeration made some bishops cautious, and there was opposition from the older generation among people and clergy who had heard wild stories about self-appointed reformers and innovators. Some people tried to construe an incompatibility between extraliturgical, so-called popular devotions and liturgical prayer, fearing from their own legalistic attitude toward liturgy that a cold and soulless piety might destroy what they thought to be the real food for Catholic souls. But this never happened. From time to time, certain ascetic schools have objected to the "free and easy" ascetism built on this less methodical and less technical attitude toward sanctification and have uttered grumbling warnings. But they underestimated the sound religious schooling of the leaders, who had an older tradition to defend than these men of the *Devotio Moderna* and the nineteenth century.

Those hard-working men, Abbot Herwegen, Dom Hammenstede, and Dom Casel with their confrères, and with the assistance of other orders, priests and laymen, threw open the doors of the sanctuary to God's people, a chosen generation, a kingly priesthood, a holy nation to offer up spiritual sacrifices.

DENVER AND MARIA LAACH

In the United States the groundwork of the liturgical weeks was laid by Dom Michael Ducey. He had studied the different liturgical movements in Austria, Belgium, and Germany, and returned to this country with a deep conviction that this was the cause to which he must dedicate himself. He succeeded after many labors, one can say single-handedly, first in convincing the abbots of the American Benedictines of both Congregations that some kind of *semaines liturgiques* similar to the Belgian institution of thirty years' standing was needed in this country. And he was wise enough not to copy these *semaines* slavishly, but to give them that typical American flavor of direct action and practical approach that was inevitable if he was to succeed.

The first Liturgical "Weeks" followed the idea of spreading the basic notions of the liturgy and its implications for parish and daily life. These six years were not lost. The twentieth century Catholic on the whole knows appallingly little about the sacramental life of his Church, and sees less in his parish churches, above all in America. Many a Catholic, with his proverbial obedience and strong sense of loyalty, accepts the liturgy as one of many obligations—nothing to wax enthusiastic about, a precious heritage of ages that reveled in them.

It is Father Ducey's merit to have driven a wedge into the hard shell of shallow observance with his persistent and courageous labors for his Liturgical Weeks. He and Dom Virgil Michel were the two Benedictine pioneers of a renascence that will tell only in a generation or two. Both men—the late Dom Virgil Michel, founder of *Orate Fratres* and creator of a genuinely American movement, and Dom Michael Ducey, instigator of its natural sequel and the organ for further propaganda, the Liturgical Weeks—were schooled in Europe. In their lives there towers the image of that man who shares with Dom Prosper Guéranger and Cardinal Ildefonso

Schuster the glory of having been the master of liturgy and monasticism: Abbot Ildefonse Herwegen, their equal in importance, ahead of them in deep historical intuition and consistence of thought.

When his loyal monks of St. Paul's Priory in Keyport, New Jersey, sent me the notice of his long-expected death, I found it hard to write all the things that ought to be said. As one of his pupils—over a lifetime—and an oblate of his ancient abbey on the lake, I knew him almost as well as his monks did. And yet, I feel I have no right to tell what they can do so much better, about the father on whom they have the first claim. But then, how can you write about the liturgical movement without at least mentioning him?

There were the many intimate traits that made the abbot lovable, and then there was the profound depth of personality that spread awe and reverence about him, so that you had to see it all in the one living personality to understand his charm. Was he greater in his miter and crozier, singing the mysteries of Christ in the sacred liturgy as I have never seen any other pontiff do it: his clear, chaste, and beautiful voice, the measured nobility of his gestures, the almost visible recollection and the complete absence of any affectation, suggesting a consecrated humanism, a sweetness of Christ that was almost tangible? Or was he greater as the father of his monks, the learned expert in monastic, liturgical, and juridical history, the rule of St. Benedict incarnate, the attentive host and listener, the witty yet profound *causeur* who kept his monks or any audience under an unbroken spell, hour after hour? He was as much at ease talking to an emperor as to his newest, most humble lay brother, with a learned bishop as with a young freshman. Not a tall man with an aquiline profile, but a slight man of virile grace and bearing who wore a miter without ever creating an impression of pompous vanity, a born prelate. His clear blue eyes, his high forehead, his expressive hands, and his rapid step are things you never forget. With it all went a fine sense of humor with not a trace of frivolity, vulgarity, or coarseness.

There is a story about Abbot Herwegen that gives an idea of the impression he made. He always wore the simple habit of the Benedictines and a plain silver pectoral cross. Yet one day when he entered Cologne Cathedral in a procession with the archbishop, a sharp-eyed young cleric remarked: "There they are, His Eminence of Cologne and His Elegance of Maria Laach."

It is impossible to give even a rough idea of his tremendous influence in the many fields of Catholic life or to mention the innumerable monks to whom he gave a fuller, more truly Benedictine idea of monasticism. With his singular intuition of history he has probably inspired more historical theses in the minds of scholars than anyone who was not a professor of history.

The Church of the Fathers and the ages of creative liturgies, Roman and Eastern, the heroic age of his order, were his great love. It was he who put Dom Odo Casel, one of his own monks, in the path of research that brought to light the heart and core of a new and more adequate understanding of the liturgy, the concept of the sacraments as "cult mysteries"—strangely paralleled in England by Abbot Anscar Vonier's unearthing of a similar concept in St. Thomas's theology. He it was who held the first Liturgical Week in Maria Laach in 1914, who inaugurated the famous collection, "Ecclesia Orans," that gave the German liturgical movement its singular profundity and solidity. He was the cause of that unique enterprise, "Annals of Liturgical Research," and a number of other scholarly enterprises that were the inexhaustible well from which others drew water: Pius Parsch in his great movement of popularization in Austria, Switzerland, and Germany; Dom Virgil Michel in his clear grasp of the American movement; the new French liturgical movement, the second wave after the impact of Solesmes had quieted down; the German youth movement which showed its liturgical fruit even in our American prisoner-of-war camps; and finally the liturgical movement in Italy, not to speak of the sister abbeys in Germany who accepted him as their foremost leader and emulated his monks in a new fervor, adding shades and variations to his great and monumental conceptions. And all of this was transmitted by his consecrated personality that in sermons and homilies rose to hymn-like grandeur. The secret of his vast influence seems to have been that from the gestures of his hands to the style of speech and the form of his thought everything expressed the perfect monk and abbot of St. Benedict.

To have had a man to incarnate the ideas and aims of the rebirth of the liturgy is the pride of the German liturgical movement, a parent movement of our own. It prevented it from being beset with the curse of a lunatic fringe or of those externalists whose greatest worry is forever the lace alb, the correct pronunciation of Latin, and the withdrawal of their own élite from coarse reality, something that has contributed so much to the general misconception that prevails among clergy and layfolk. We often regretted that he had no diocese to reform, but now that he is gone, I think we are glad that he was spared from being wasted in chancery routine, administrative troubles, and frustrations due to the sheer inertia of his flock.

Our own American liturgical movement is indebted to him in a way that leaves it free from the slavery of pure imitation, because Dom Virgil Michel was enough of a realist to see that with all the elemental and basic agreement he felt with Abbot Herwegen, our land demanded its own version born of definite national and local necessities. We are deeply indebted to him for this. Abbot Herwegen, for example, could not conceive of a place for the vernacular in the liturgy. To him the vague, complex, and rebellious German mind and its "formlessness" needed the lucidity, constraint, and majesty of Latin as an educating factor. Even in Germany Pius Parsch courageously took another road, and today a number of German dioceses administer most sacraments in the vernacular and have as much of it in the Mass as is feasible, clamoring for more. After the first abortive attempt of the late Father Campbell of Halifax, Nova Scotia, to discuss this matter, in 1909, Dom Virgil was the first one to call for a greater measure of English in our liturgy. In many other ways he maintained his independence, above all in his firm stand on the social implications of the liturgy, his restless fight for the social encyclicals, and his steadfast rejection of that troublesome misconception that tries to confuse the Kingdom of God with some "Sacral

Empire," and Christ's Headship with a claim to monarchic forms of state life. Dom Michel was as good a disciple of Maritain as he was of Abbot Herwegen.

The Belgian Liturgical Movement, which under the leadership of Dom Lambert Beauduin was primarily a pastoral movement, also strongly influenced Dom Virgil Michel. These influences, added to his own independence of mind, enabled Dom Michel to bring into being the organized liturgical movement in this country in 1926 when the Liturgical Press was established by the American Benedictines at Collegeville, Minnesota, and the first issue of *Orate Fratres* appeared.

The 1946 meeting in Denver marked the first tentative steps into a new kind of liturgical realism. The time for fundamentals and generalities is over. Concrete tasks have to be mastered. The bishops, the clergy, and the laity want to see what the liturgy means to do for every one of us. If we can't show this, it will remain an esoteric pasture for esthetes, intellectuals, and pious conventicles.

The great problem of our days is the restoration of our families, which either have already become, or are on the verge of being, atomized. The Church combats birth control and fights further secularization of the family. Labor unions, church agencies, and political parties lead an uphill fight for restoration of the family's economic, social, and political climate. The inroads of the present plague of divorce are extreme. To conjure the "good old days" or the "average American family" or Judge Hardy movies is a poor way of conveying an ideal. Nor is a mere declamation of the idyl of Nazareth so effective—too little is known in detail of that life and few women dare "realize" in their minds the equation between themselves and Our Blessed Lady. Nor do the other equations, pious, idyllic, romantic, as they are, have a particular appeal to young American couples and their offspring! I wonder whether the late medieval invention of this technique by the epigones of Eckhart, Suso, and *"Devotio Moderna"* was an all-round blessing! Greater realism is needed.

The Denver Liturgical Week attempted this Christian realism

from its loftiest definitions to its most common details. Once the partial notions of modern popular devotionalism are outgrown, and the wholeness of the Church's sacramental cosmos is seen, this new realism becomes again possible. The realism of which I speak is one of faith—faith in its fullness, with less emphasis on the mere defensive interest that we inherited than a full grasp of the supernatural as the great Fathers saw the new cosmos descended to earth in Christ. In this faith, certainly, all things are made new.

The mere pious verbiage on matrimony as a mystery in Christ and the Church is then discarded for a real grasp that man and wife are in a true, real relationship to each other as Christ and His Church, that marriage is a continuous bearer and channel of divine life, ministered by the other partner, as Dom Godfrey Diekmann showed. The elaboration of this reality took a whole day and six papers in three sessions. Pastors and married men and women showed by very definite examples the application of the great truths. So many Catholics who feel that their marriage, above the purely natural level, is nothing but an empty plateau with fences of commands and prohibitions all round, realized the enormous riches, the positive charge, and the fertility of this plateau once the waters of the sacrament had irrigated it.

A talk given by Mary Perkins Ryan climaxed the "week." When she spoke of her chores, her cooking recipes, her life as a mother, wife, housewife, and writer, one perceived one life in which sacramental realism had come true. The complete absence of affectation and of popular pseudo-liturgies imported from Europe's peasantries or small-town bourgeois showed for once that you can be a modern American and liturgical without becoming touchingly weird and strange. The hundreds of sisters and priests who heard the full doctrine and liturgical richness must have realized how much there is to do to free our teaching from that pseudo-claustral anemia which besets so much of our catechesis on this great sacrament. There was a member of the articulate laity—putting us clerics to shame—the only hope for any Catholic Action. Married people all over the United

States ought to know what took place at this first "penetrative" Liturgical Week that broke with spiritual isolationism.

Bourgeois Catholicism did not even improve the bourgeoisie. What good does it do if secular magazines in a mood that oscillates between irony and a sort of respect give a kind of left-handed publicity to careers of prelates or what they think to be medieval expressions of faith? Where do demonstrations, parades, resolutions, and clamorings lead us? Is it really worth while to be regarded as a major pressure group in the tug of war with all the rest? What consolation do we get from (mostly arbitrary) statistics? What do we accomplish by backing any cause that has a Catholic label, without further investigation? Even if we succeed in attaining a certain standing, can we always go on feeding on others' grudging respect or even admiration, while the sacramental life has been thinned down to a trickle in a jungle of emotional growth all over the Church year?

Have you ever seen and heard a cathedral full of priests, sisters, and lay people sing an archbishop's Mass together as one man? In Denver it happened, though fortunately not for the last time. In the evening hundreds chanted the psalms and hymns of Compline together. Remembering your own parish church, you will believe me: there is spiritual spring in the air right now in our own country.

2

The Work of the People

A SOCIAL LEAVEN?

Catholics and Protestant Christians outside the Anglo-Saxon orbit often blame us English-speaking Catholics for being "activists." The classical case was the heresy of "Americanism" at the turn of the century. It is a common assumption of the more profound Christian critics in Latin, Slavic, and Teutonic countries of the old Continent, and perhaps also in Latin America and Asia, that Catholicism in the Anglo-Saxon countries (not to speak of Protestantism) has lost an element of Christianity which is best expressed by the word "contemplative" although this term is as unfit to cover the whole complex as any other would be. There is much more involved than just contemplation itself.

It is the whole mood of cultural and civilizational optimism to which objection is taken. To these observers our "version" of Christ's religion, has all but—the cross. To them we, especially we in America, seem to fall into the ancient trap of millenarianism, confusing Jesus' message of spiritual redemption with earthly prosperity, and seeing in His life, since He rose from the dead, a rewarding "success story," while forgetting that His resurrection was, though a historical fact, in a new "aion" not accessible to mortal man in his life.

Our critics feel that the optimism with which we aggressively tackle the world to make it over is shallow and is the result of another shortcoming: a disregard for truth, for doctrine, for clarity. In their eyes we are so eager to go out and get going that we lose sight of the primacy of the "logos" over the "ethos" (to quote Guardini).

And the result? The paradoxes of life, the intellectual mystery surrounding all matters of faith, are ignored, soft-pedaled: the "obscure light" becomes a very trite, banal, and obvious thing, as it were a neon tube substituting for the sun.

Anglo-Saxon Christianity, even in its Catholic form, appears to all the rest of the world as entirely too practical, too efficient, too ethical a thing to be commendable. It is too fond of immediate results, of statistics, of building programs and pat answers, and too easily satisfied with solutions. Our critics fear that in centuries to come so much of the practical, Protestant ethos will have been assimilated that we will become a "do-gooding," charitable service organization, with a dogma and liturgy on a level with the weird ritual of Masons and Shriners and a moral code like a libertine perversion of Methodism or Lutheranism.

Reinhold Niebuhr once stated that we live in a country where churches become sects and sects churches. By this he meant, if I understood him rightly, that even the majesty and universality of the Catholic Church are hard to assert in our climate: for the smallest group of crackpots and fanatics not only (and justly) finds the right to speak and teach, but because the majesty of tradition, of an integrated structure of doctrine, of well defined laws and discipline, of cultural accomplishment count for nothing in the face of zeal and aggressiveness is accepted without credentials as an equal, or worse, as a foreign, strange, and dangerous "sect."

How long will Catholics be able to maintain their claim in this climate? Are the devices now used, often borrowed from others, like the publicity we so generously achieve, sufficient? Are we really made for competition in an atmosphere of Bible-quoting puritanism? Is the claim of having answers others do not have sufficient? These are questions that worry the responsible leaders.

After this introduction one might come to the conclusion: If all this be so, if we need something to offset our alleged activism, our optimism so purely spiritual, then, as a part of a whole, our liturgical movement is one of the best antidotes. For what could be more antiutilitarian than to express worship of God in solemnity?

What could heal us more from Pelagian self-perfection, trust in human activity and achievement, than the freely given graces of the sacraments?

Yet more: Why bring in sociological references which will only make it appear as if even the liturgy is being used to bolster activism? Let us restore the liturgy in its fullness to the people, as outlined by our Holy Father, and social action will flow from it quite naturally— as someone has said not long ago. If activism is our peculiar danger (and Guardini's words, written back in 1918, show that it is a very real danger even to our critics in Europe), is it wise to provide it with another source?

I think that chance must be taken. It would be utterly unrealistic not to do so. We all know of daily communicants who fail to be a witness in their circles and whose only mark of lived religion seems to be their daily Holy Communion and what it involves. They are in good faith. They are earnest. They make great sacrifices by going to Communion and by "staying in the state of grace" week after week, year after year. One cannot track down the workings of grace and their nearness to God; their transformation into members of Christ cannot be registered under microscopes or with chemico-electric waves on charts. Something is bound to happen to them and to those with whom they live, on which their daily divine repast has had a determining influence. But still: the quietism latent in their attitude, unknown to themselves, frustrates the fullest effectiveness of the Holy Eucharist. In a bold image: it is like high-octane gas in a broken-down one-cylinder motor.

After all, grace presupposes and perfects nature. Which means, reversed, that we are obliged to "work on nature" and do what we can to give grace a broader, deeper, and more sensitive surface to tackle. And this involves not only, as activism wants us to believe, the ennobling of will and emotions, but also the broadening and deepening of our natural knowledge. Thomas à Kempis' statement that it is better to have contrition than to be able to define it is only good as far as it goes: to have contrition plus the most profound knowledge of true contrition is better still! There is an objective scale of values in the realm of being that many spiritual writers disregard for the sake of pouring comfort into the hearts of those whose invincible ignorance needs comforting.

If then there are sociological and social implications in our sacramental system as embodied in our liturgy, we should make much of them! The bride-and-groom relationship of the soul and Jesus in Communion, or the aspect of divine visitation in the Holy Eucharist, are certainly sublime ideals for any soul, and highly commendable. But that is not all there is to it! The Lord's Supper is also, even primarily, a banquet and a sacrifice. That the altar rail is full of people like myself is not just accidental, but part and parcel of the visible sign, signifying a reality of this sacrament. The poor at my side must be an alarm to me. If the colored parishioners are discriminated against, the sacrament must inflame me. The beauty of the liturgy and its sacred order must be a thorn in my side if at the same time the socio-economic order of my country is a mockery of the Gospel and if Christ's friends, the poor, are ignored while the well washed, well dressed, well housed and respectable are given practical preference as the "good" Catholics.

Justice and charity cannot be excluded: the liturgy carried out to perfection, not only exteriorly, but even with the knowledge and spiritual disposition striven after by the best liturgists, will be a tinkling cymbal in the ears of God unless the ones who celebrate it continue to glorify the same Lord in the economic, social, political, and cultural fields.

These implications simply don't take care of themselves. The sacraments challenge our whole nature: body, will, reason. If we were Quakers we might be satisfied with God in our hearts only and exclusively—although *they* aren't, as their good deeds show. But since we are members of that Mystical Body which prolongs the Incarnation, the state of the body social is a liturgical concern.

So in the name of Baptism and Confirmation, of Penance, of Eucharist and Holy Orders, of Matrimony and of the Unction for eternal glory, in the name of their garb of prayers, rites, and readings, we who claim to live by them must be found in the forefront of those who work for a new society built according to the justice and charity of Christ.

Of course, no confusion of function is intended: housing, care of health, interracial justice, the living wage and family subsidies are not topics for Liturgical Weeks. Nor is it a directly liturgical concern to decide whether "free enterprise" can exist the Roepke-Hayek-Mises way, or whether a society compounded of social and individual ownership is the solution for our complex social age. These are questions for the Social Action movement, to be solved according to the progressively developed teaching of papal encyclicals. But a disinterested liturgical movement, or even a mildly concerned one, would be as worthy of suspicion as the one castigated in *Mediator Dei* as archaic. One ought not to demand more participation for the people, more ways for the laity to share in the conscious celebration of Christ's mysteries, unless it makes us better Christians. And this means that we have a concern, or rather, an anxiety in our heart, to see all realms of life permeated by the Savior's Spirit.

Whether the New-Deal-like legislation of the past or another method to establish the brotherhood of man is right is subject to debate. But to withdraw into a fools' paradise fenced in by rubrics, and to tend vestments and rites, to give blessings to things of the earth without making them serve the just and right way, cannot be debated: it is wrong.

Dom Virgil Michel and the movement inspired by his leadership saw this from the beginning, and the movement never lost itself in romantic dreams of sacral empires, of societies made up of sacred estates, of crowns and coronations. It looked forward, well knowing that Utopia would never become real and that the kingdom of Christ fully realized is an event, not of the year A.D. 2000 or 3000, but of the post-parousia. As in the lives of the saints, it is not the achievements but the heroic degree of virtue with which we strive that constitutes our task.

Between shallow activism and naïve optimism, this-worldly and natural, on the one hand, and, on the other, awareness of our duty to lay down our lives for justice and charity's sake in order to implement what we do in sacred signs, there is a world of difference. The same men and women who beg for more vernacular, who strive for sanctity through a more intense living in the sacramental world of the liturgy and through their ascetic efforts, must be the ones who not only give alms—person to person or in drives—but who help unions, sit on employers' councils and housing committees, in interracial groups and Catholic Action centers, who campaign for medical services for the strata that cannot afford them, who oppose demagoguery and injustice to the freedoms needed by man, and make the cause of enslaved nations a matter of their own heart. It is not much use to shout about the "collective tendencies" in industrial society if we don't want to pay the price for a more individualistic form, which is a lower standard of living. That means that we must not be content with consecrating individuals; we must now tackle whole groups and promote the concept of justice that necessarily accompanies this new situation.

A refusal to do so would amount to setting the clock back. A Christian who looks forward to the parousia cannot act thus.

THUNDERSTORM RELIGION

We hear a great deal about the shrinking of the religious sphere in human lives. I am not talking about our fellow Christians whose entire religious practice consists in appearing in church to be "hatched, matched, and dispatched." The Church has always had them with her, like the physically poor. Nor do I allude to that ever-growing number of men and women, young and old, who seem to have been born without a *potentia obedientialis,* in plain English, without an organ for religion. They are often nice and decent people, yet they seem to be incarnate ghosts of an order different from our own. They give you a blank stare when you indicate that faith and religious practice mean more to you than just a lovable or detestable whim of your mind.

I am talking about sincerely practicing Catholics and other

religious people who believe in God and a supernatural end and aim of our lives. Even their religion has shrunk extensively, and in a dozen different ways.

Their prayer life, once rich and all-embracing, is now reduced to a set of half a dozen formulas. They can't speak to God unless they recite and repeat Our Fathers and Hail Marys. God is the "great bureaucrat" to whom you submit your applications, which appear the more urgent the longer they are. You must see forms stabilized by tradition and custom. You don't sing hymns and psalms to God, nor do you use the language of your own heart. We have become religiously inarticulate.

Still another shrinkage and impoverishment can be observed: the language of most of our devotions has become poor because of over-statement, superlatives, and the tendency to be effusive and gushy. Its province has narrow boundaries of feeling, narrower boundaries of reason, and no cosmic character at all. Most of our devotions speak the language and think the thoughts of the eighteenth century. Al-most all of our hymns are on the sentimental side.

A more serious shrinkage is that of dogmatic consciousness. We live on a few crumbs from the table of tradition and revelation. Moralism and pragmatism have overtaken us, in spite of a certain counteremphasis by men like Karl Adam, de Lubac, Guardini, and Rahner. Those aspects of our sacraments that fit into this picture of moralism and pragmatism, symptoms of a bourgeois mind, are the only ones we appreciate. The loftier ones, born from a rich and full appreciation of the whole sacramental system, are gone to live a paper life in dogma books.

Naturally this has happened to our liturgy too. Most of the *Pontificale* and *Rituale,* the *Graduale* and *Vesperale* is never done or sung. All we have is some field baggage in a knapsack, while the trunks are locked in a dusty attic. We go up there once in a while to look at them. We point to these hidden and forgotten treasures for apologetic reasons, but we don't *use* them. A half-hour for Mass, which is no longer a solemn rite of celebration but either a show or a commodity for our subjective complement or a means of acquiring something for ourselves, together with some abbreviated daily prayers, a few concentrated attacks on ourselves in missions, retreats, parades, novenas, and mammoth congresses—these are our modern substitutes for the rich, organic life that embraced and carried our ancestors to eternal glory.

Why is this so? Because we are disoriented. Religion has unwittingly been dislocated. It is not so much bad will, lack of interest, or intentional disregard. It began long ago. The sphere of the supernatural has been shriveling in our minds and, since acting always follows being, it shrank in our practical lives too. The materialist says that religion is only a childish attempt to explain and endure nature. According to him science has done away with its necessity. Man understands now that a thunderstorm is a purely natural thing, a discharge of electricity, aero-physics, and what not, and not a grandiose manifestation of God's anger. A flash of lightning neither hits arbitrarily nor is it a moral weapon of God's justice. We don't yet know the complicated formula for every individual flash but we know the general theory.

What seemed to be a very moody thing, the weather, is something that ultimately is governed by iron laws and hard facts: the stars, air, electricity, pressures, the sun, and a thousand other factors determine it with iron necessity. It only seems to be whimsical. It really is very reasonable, and if we knew all its components and were able to weigh and measure them, we could predict the weather for July 4, 1972. God is not constantly meddling with it, they say. He will not change it because the sodality has a picnic, or the parish has a procession, or Hitler needs it for a show or a battle. To our fathers nature was not only a revelation of God's wisdom, beauty, power, goodness, and justice, but it shared His supernatural, superrational "mysteriosity" in some way. Then came the age of science, and the "mystery" began its retreat. Everything became an object of chemistry, physics, astronomy, and mathematics. Now we can make gold out of iron, at least theoretically, without being suspected of having the devil as our partner.

Psychoanalysis did the rest. Even the functions of dreams have been recognized. Of course, a great deal of misinterpretation has occurred. Freud was wrong in many things, but on the whole his thesis has been accepted even by Christian psychology.

Thus "secularism" has superseded what I should like to call good old thunderstorm religion. We seem to need God for only so few things nowadays, the things we can't cope with ourselves: moral failure, metaphysical blues, and cultural hangovers. The more we know, the less we seem to need Him. Thus our religious consciousness and practice, our popular piety and pulpit theology, lag sadly behind our times. Everywhere we seem to be on the defensive, losing ground not only in public but also in the souls of our faithful. We retreat further and further, become more and more minimalistic in every respect, hoping secretly that this will blow over as did Nero's persecution, the migration of nations, the Dark Ages, heresies, and revolutions. We seem to say: "Let us just sit tight, and through sheer force of numbers, through tradition and inertia, we shall simply outlive them. They are dying out anyhow, through birth control, at a faster rate than we. We still have some brakes to rely on that they do not have. The siege will be over someday." I don't say that this is a conscious strategic plan of action, but it seems to be a subconscious certainty: it happened before. "The gates of hell, and so on . . ." Some of us meet the situation differently by resentment and escape: science is no good, overrated, uncertain, contradictory. We are romantics and medievalists. The golden age once was; it will come again. Nicolai Berdyaev and others sell us this theory, thinking, of course, of the great features of that era: its art, its philosophy, its saints, and its "world conception," closed, rational, secure, well integrated in faith and God. But although they call it "new," it is all an attempt to set the clock back because we are late.

We do not want it. It would be distrust in the power of the Kingdom of God. It would be a sin against the Spirit. Science has brought us truths, and even purely natural truth makes us free. Christ consecrated the universe through His advent. This world consecration has to go on. We cannot lay down our tools and weapons because we are tired of the breath-taking advance of progress, because of the tragic and sanguinary failures it constantly suffers, or because we have lost our orientation and have reduced religion to a commodity serving those aspects of life that progress *as yet* does not satisfy. Mere "salvation religion" degenerates into its own shadow of being an escape. Religion's consecratory and sacerdotal aspect has to be reinstated to disprove agnosticism and materialism. Present-day Catholicism is awakening, but is not yet really alive to its task. The Popes have indicated the general direction, but the Church responds only slowly. The liturgical movement is its most profound and radical response. It involves a fundamental change and frees us from our present negative attitude, our minimalism in doctrine, our insincere, halfhearted attitude toward true progress, our *ressentiment*, our lack of rational orientation. If we are not able to warm the new, cold, immense universe science has discovered with our faith and charity, we shall have failed our times. A brave, new faith and charity are necessary, built on the original mysteries of Christ.

THE DEXTERITY OF MISSING THE POINT

It is hard to remember the many witty and trenchant remarks of Chesterton, but I seem to recollect his saying somewhere: "It is remarkable how some people have an unfailing ability to miss the point." He may have said this in a mood of exasperation while he tried to make a point with some dissident brother on a matter of Catholic doctrine. But you don't have to be a heretic to have this ability—there are plenty of people among our own who are endowed with this striking and bewildering talent. Nobody defending the basic or even marginal aspects of the liturgical movement can long remain unaware of this.

There is the good man who inveighs against altars facing the people. As I understand it, taught by those who are experts in rubrical matters, the problem is simple. The general rubrics of the missal consider such an altar as one of the two possibilities. Historically, at least in Rome whence we received our own liturgy, this position seems to be older than our present custom, but neither could be called the "correct" one in an exclusive way; for there are good reasons and established tradition for each. It is obviously the right of the local ordinary to decide which is more appropriate in our day and will serve the people and the liturgy best.

But there seemingly is no end to fighting the altar facing the people with arguments such as: the Holy See frowns on the practice (which would, incidentally, put the Holy Father under the embarrassing obligation of frowning for hours every time he descends to one of his basilicas to sing Holy Mass). Or the other one, that you need permission from Rome. Or the one that it detracts from the celebrant's devotion (which presupposes that the average priest regards the Mass as his private and intimate devotion).

The weightiest argument is always that of *"admiratio populi"* (astonishment of the faithful), understood as if you should always leave the churchgoing public with the comfortable idea that there is no better way of doing things than the way they are being done. But there is also a good *"admiratio populi,"* created by the proper authority as was the case when Pope Pius X advanced the age of first Communion, and when Pius XII gave us psalms we could understand, the power to confirm in emergencies, the new Holy Week, and other things that made people reflect and ask questions. The argument for or against, in the matter of the altar facing the people, is solely one of expediency and proper procedure. All others bark up the wrong tree.

The vernacular movement runs into the same sort of argumentation. Answered a hundred times, someone who has never heard the argument will parade the same old hobbyhorses as others before him. Among them is sure to be the one that goes something like this: "It is painful to listen to the average priest's hasty pronunciation, and luckily most of them whisper so they do not disturb the devotion of the attendants. Now just imagine some priest bellowing the English text from the altar, possibly with a French or German accent or a juicy Irish brogue."

Then there is what the late Father Gosling called the argument "*ex tourismo,*" in other words: When you go to China you will hear the familiar (*sic!*) Latin and feel at home at once (probably because you understand about as much of it as of Chinese). Or, to mention the other horn of the dilemma: What will the English-speaking priest do when he travels in Iraq or Sicily? Although we never dreamed of suggesting that Rome forbid the use of Latin missals, but only that the mother tongue be permitted for those parts of the Mass that are meant for the congregation at parish Mass and in parishes only, the opponents always assume that the vernacularists want to pour out the baby with the bath. A Latin missal will come into its own in such a case: the traveling priest will use it for his private Mass. Seems sensible and simple to me.

Hardly has this been explained, then out come all the other reasons: the everlasting claim that the Mass is a mystery and therefore demands a dead, mysterious language. Why this should apply to collect, gospel, and epistle I for one cannot see. Then comes the claim that Latin is a necessary safeguard of unity. That the use of Latin in the liturgy is "a manifest and beautiful sign of unity . . . in a considerable portion of the Church" is clear enough, and has been explicitly stated by the Holy Father (*Mediator Dei*, n. 60). But it is equally clear that the Eucharist, the sacraments, and the Creed, not even mentioning the Holy See itself, are the really necessary and effective symbols of unity. Else, what about the Catholics of Greek, Old Slavonic, and other rites? Some insist that Latin in itself is sacred, more musical, and better adapted to worship than any modern language. This is very much a matter of personal opinion and would hardly stand close scrutiny. Or do we really claim that the Lord's Prayer in English is not as sacred as in a foreign and obsolete tongue?

It would be a waste of time to continue. When Rome changed from Greek to Latin, it changed from the language of the few to the language of the many, in other words, to vernacular. Since the Holy See has officially declared that a partial use of the mother tongue in the liturgy is beneficial, there is only one *problem* involved: the problem of making the change in the right fashion: and it is on this score that we can have sensible arguments and exciting ones. We should argue about the amount of vernacular, the quality of the translation, the way to prepare the people for a change, the replacing of spurious and obsolete reasons for Latin in our catechisms with more adequate ones (for example, tradition), the best manner of making our wishes known to our hierarchy, and the mode of transition.

The problem, as I see it, is big enough without sham arguments. The departure from a tradition of sixteen hundred years and the thorny question of making the right change at the right time and in the right way constitute formidable tasks: granted. But I personally feel that the reasons for the change and against all-Latin are more urgent and that Rome knows well enough how to make changes prudently. But I am willing to discuss the merits of true arguments. What bothers me is the dexterity with which so many miss the point and drag in unreasonable reasons.

This same attitude comes to mind every time I instruct a convert concerning the Holy Eucharist. There are, thank God, always those who scrutinize what they are being offered and who want reasons. Their argument is then: "Father, Jesus said in Matthew, 'All of you drink of this,' and in Mark it says, 'they all drank of it,' and St. Paul (1 Cor. 11:25) definitely states that this 'cup is the new covenant in my blood; do this. . . .'" (The text of our missal follows the explicit command of St. Matthew: "Take and drink ye all of it.")

Father Yves Congar, O.P., in his great work *True and False Reform in the Church,* says that the use of the chalice for the people "was not a question of dogma, and the Holy See will end by allowing the use of the chalice." And yet, when you look at the average catechism, this point of discipline and expediency is made a point of dogma. The use of the chalice was never "abolished" by any decree. Like all such changes, it came about as gradually as a geological change. Reasons were many, among them a shift of dogmatic emphasis, but this was hardly the most powerful driving force. And yet it would seem that way, when you read our ordinary means of instruction. If you say that the *reason* for giving Communion under one species only is that Christ is present, whole and entire, under the species of bread, you will once in a while get the puzzled question: "Then why did Jesus institute two species and add the command to drink?" The answer that two species were needed for the Sacrifice but not for Communion is a reasonable one and will be accepted; but is it the best we can do?

The true reasons, the historical ones, were those of convenience and reverence (difficulty in administering the sacrament to large crowds, fear of spilling the sacred species, and some others). These reasons could never have prevailed had not the dogmatic emphasis on the background truth—as developed during the age of scholasticism—conditioned the minds for a change. When rebellious minds like Hus, Wycliffe, Luther, Zwingli, and Calvin linked this question with heresy and schism, what Father Congar calls the "rightist" and the "Spanish" attitude prevailed, and the Church protected the recent tradition as legitimate.

Moreover, the partial theology that concerns itself largely with the Real Presence, an emphasis thrust on the Church by heresies, is not the complete approach to this mystery. Eucharist as banquet, as sacrifice, as the center of the Mystical Body, is much wider and larger, and in this wider and larger view the real proportions are restored.

No loyal Catholic will doubt the power of the Church to rule and govern. If the Church saw fit to withhold one species of the Blessed Sacrament for valid reasons (as she previously had substituted the less onerous baptism by pouring for the fuller rite of immersion), a loyal son of the Church accepts this disciplinary change. But it is an unenlightened and poor conception of loyalty to use dogmatic arguments to justify what may be temporary. Once a thing is dogmatically established, no Pope or general council can restore the initial state. Could Pius X have restored the true conception of the Holy Eucharist if infrequent Communion had been based on dogmatic reasons instead of discipline?

The Church is not a fossil, but a living organism. Nor is she a skeleton, but a Body with a skeleton, if one may use this image. She lives, and a living organism adapts itself. Should the Holy See judge that the twentieth century Catholic needs an even fuller Eucharist and would be more deeply immersed in Eucharistic spirit by partaking of both species of the sacred banquet, an appeal to the wrong reasons now would make it practically impossible to adjust the sacramental practice to the potential demands of sacramental completeness. It is perhaps beside the point that under each of the species we have the complete Christ—a truth no Christian doubts: the point may be the completeness of signification.

A concatenation of historical causes in which dogmatic links provided firm support brought about this change. We should defend the right of the Church to adapt discipline to successive ages, but if we try to prove too much we do harm. Therefore we should leave the dogmatic justification in right proportion. Otherwise we are not only right for the wrong reasons, but commit the Apostolic See to positions only the Pope and a general council can take up. We should not forget that perfectly orthodox Catholics in union with Rome to this day give both species and that any Latin Catholics may go to Holy Communion in such churches; that the chalice in some instances was given to the people as late as the late fifteenth century; that the Council of Trent even allowed reintroduction of this use in Austria and other countries for a time; and that the rubric, prescribing the chalice of ablution for the laity—though now out of use and obsolete—is still in our books.

To be sure the issues mentioned above—the vernacular, the altar facing the people, and the very remote and in-actual question of the two species—are brought in for arguing the point that many people attack issues for the wrong reasons. The liturgical movement in America has made none of these issues its own. The last one has not even been mentioned, nor, to be truthful, even been thought of. I could have brought up popular participation in high Mass or dialogue Mass just as well. But I felt these three instances were more illuminating than any others, and apt illustrations of "dexterity in missing the point."

A CHANGE OF EMPHASIS

The number of individuals receiving Communion has doubtlessly risen since the day on which Pius X promulgated his famous Communion decrees. You see it at weekday Masses in our cities. You see evergrowing crowds thronging the altar rails on first Fridays. You have a goodly number of regular communicants on Sundays. Of course, not even the smuggest observer could say that we are anywhere near the ideal Communion of all who participate in Mass. But will that ever be attained?

In spite of all this visible progress, if we look closer, we see something disturbing. It is that these regular communicants, on the whole, approach the sacred banquet not for reasons intrinsically evident from the very banquet itself, nor from their family status. Since this is a point of great subtlety and hard to break down into palatable morsels of thought, permit me to indulge in a few sweeping generalizations. I may have to say a few uncommon things. Allow me to take you over a rough road, away from the slick and smooth everyday highways of complacency and routine.

To state it bluntly: we have no family Communion because we have organized the family to pieces and done with our parishes exactly what modern individualism in its capitalistic and communistic shades has done to society, mind you, against our protest and our loud outcries. At least, that is the case as far as our Eucharistic practice is concerned. The father of the family goes to Communion with the Holy Name Society, the Knights of Columbus, and now also with veteran groups. These occasions are "sold to the men" as demonstrations of faith, an inspiration for the ones who sit and watch. Is this not a rather peculiar motive to eat and drink the Flesh and Blood of the Lamb of God? And the mother goes with her Altar Society or Mothers' Club, and on first Fridays, not so much to inspire the gaping crowds in the last pews, but because the pastor expects her to do so, and because she has a motherly urge to do so to obtain blessings and grace for her family.

What about the grown or growing son? If he is in a Catholic college he is caught by the atmosphere and "goes" often, even daily. When he comes home he does a little more or less than his father, depending on such things as the organization that mothers him, or the mother he loves, or a genuine natural urge of his young manhood. (I am not, of course, mentioning those young men who have a hard time getting themselves aroused to fervor on the two principal feasts of the year.) Translate this into the feminine, and you have a similar situation. And the younger children? They are exposed to the influence of the home and the school. But many parishes have no parochial school, and therefore the impact of the home is stronger than that of a catechism class. Summer vacations show a remarkable drop in children's Communions!

We selected what we felt to be the best cases, but it has left us with the family as an institution that breeds children, feeds them, farms them out for education, and forms a sort of moral union promoting, protecting, and guaranteeing the varying degrees of religious life of the individual members. The organizing principle of this religious life comes from outside the family. Nor does the Church year help to develop a rhythm into these different timetables of spirituality. Of course, you may ask, who wants a rhythm? Or why interfere with something as personal as an individual's relationship to his Maker? This question would do honor to a Quaker or Pietist. Unless you show me that you are exceptionally honored by ecstasies and visions, I will answer: Because the family is not merely a moral, economic, and social unit; it is a living cell of Christ's Body, an organism in itself.

Sacraments are in the order of visible things, or "holy signs," as St. Thomas calls them. They were instituted by Christ as "signs," and are not just a primitive form of religion that the twentieth century has outgrown. We should leave them where Christ put them: in the world of practical symbols. The Eucharist is a banquet. If father goes to Communion, while the family watches proudly, then he is alone at the banquet, and the banquet is not a banquet of the family. How can we expect love between consorts to survive the family trials

of twenty, thirty, or more years, the withering of bodies, once young
and beautiful, the growing sclerosis of their characters, the boredom
nature engenders, unless a new and more sublime experience of love
is born in this banquet at the altar of the slain and risen Lamb?
Should not married couples come back hand in hand from the altar
of Communion?

How can we expect children to keep their loving reverence for
their parents through the period of natural adolescent rebellion, the
clash of generations, and the only too natural, critical appraisal of
a maturing mind, when they see the parents, idols of their childhood,
as faint attempts and definite failures against the outline of their
own untried ideals of maturity of body and mind? If they knelt right
and left of their parents in this sacred family banquet receiving
Christ's Body—how could they help being, not only one with them
in grace, but also in mind and feelings?

I know, of course, that all this sounds strange against the background of our modern, individualistic, and rationalized pseudo-
skepticism built up around the Holy Eucharist. Liturgical barbarisms,
such as the daughter going to Communion in Seattle for her mother
in St. Louis on Mother's Day, are well intentioned and pious usages
nobody seems to be able or even willing to stop. They seem like
straws in a wind not blowing from the liturgy but from a boundless
arbitrariness of thought, or rather thoughtless emotionalism—and all
this out of good motives.

The great French theologian Henri de Lubac, S.J., in his revolutionizing book *Corpus Mysticum,* has done the Eucharistic revival of
our days a tremendous service. Of course, it will perhaps take a generation before his thought seeps down to the average level of our
dogma books. It may take another generation or two to find it penetrating the masses of our faithful. But when Pius X restored by law
a practice—frequent Communion—which had disappeared in the
earlier Dark Ages, this practice could not have been expected to go
beyond a mere outward observance and loyal obedience. We would
have to find first what constituted the conscious doctrine in its completeness, which had made frequent Communion the ordinary thing

during the ages of the martyrs and the Fathers. For it was definitely
not Jansenism that inaugurated the custom of rare Communion.
Jansen made only worse what he found already. Long before the
Council of Trent, things had gone from bad to worse. Frequent
Communion was lost at the same time that the liturgy was lost to
the common man.

H. de Lubac was the first to investigate painstakingly exactly
what happened and why it happened. Before him the liturgists of
all countries resorted to guesses and hypotheses, which usually were
summed up in two or three general statements: the transformation
of the Hellenic and Roman Europe into a Germanic, Celtic, and Slav
domain; the new, youthful, inquisitive spirit of the turbulent age;
the influence of Aristotelian instead of Platonic thinking. So far so
good. But neither the followers of neoscholasticism nor the followers
of the great medieval traditions in dogma, morals, or mysticism liked
to be classified among those who narrowed down the emphasis of
the wide, clear, and pure stream of biblical and patristic sacramental-
ism. Many cried havoc over what they called liturgism and Bene-
dictinism. A book like Anscar Vonier's *Key to the Doctrine of the
Eucharist,* which went a long way in the right direction, was practically ignored, especially by popular preaching and devotionalism.
But Père de Lubac is not biased. He is a young spirit, a vigorous
and authentic son of Ignatius.

Abbot Vonier rediscovered the full meaning of the re-presentation
which had become the colorless term of representation. From the
strong term to the weak shadow of it was a long road, from the great
Thomas down to drab modern writings. What a difference between
the "making present-again" of Christ's sacrifice—*repraesentatio*—and
the representation of the same with its hundred helpless efforts of
so-called explanation! We have not yet felt the full impact of this
happy find in our parish life, in the common articulate faith of our
people. Abbot Vonier brought us back to St. Thomas and thus
linked us with the ample, living tradition of liturgy and theology
of the Fathers. The family assisting at Mass as of old will again be a
member of the parish celebrating as one body the mysteries of

Christ; the Mystical Body will be drawn into the sacrifice of Calvary in a real, physical, yet sacramental way.

Père de Lubac is still more searching. His book is weighted down with crushing evidence, which would take the average scholar a whole lifetime to sift. Hundreds of scholars have read the same texts. Dozens of writers have quoted them to prove this and that, or have been puzzled by their wording.

And the results? A shift of emphasis, a narrowing of vision, a shelving of rich aspects. The rich symbolism of the Fathers was practically discarded for an interest in one aspect only, the real presence of Our Lord. All the others, first shelved for argument's sake, were permanently left to the blind readings of scholars looking for props for their theses, while the people heard no more of them. Oh, yes, they were still known, but brushed aside as part of the strange, weird symbolic theology of Augustine, Ambrose, and Amalar. What could the dwarfs who burrowed in St. Thomas's mountainous structure do with it?

To come back to the main topic, let us look at the crucial problem. The theologians of the ninth century began to systemize the heritage of the Fathers and the liturgy. There is one systematic effort which, although of no theological importance, is very significant. Using the breaking into three of the host after the Our Father during Mass, Amalar distinguishes three bodies, or rather three phases of the same body of Christ; the first fragment signifies the body of Christ as it lived on earth, which was born and crucified; the second, as it is consumed by the faithful in Communion; and the third as it lives in what we call his "Mystical Body," his Church. Of course, this is not liturgy or theology, or even genuine symbolism. But it is useful to demonstrate three things:

First: Up to that time even so pedestrian a writer as Amalar was vividly conscious that the historical, the sacramental, and the ecclesial Christ are one.

Second: Before and long after this time, the sacramental Christ was called the Mystical Body. (Father de Lubac calls his whole book *Corpus Mysticum,* although it does not try to cover the territory so ably treated by Father Mersch, S.J.) This indicates a much wider idea of mysticism, a closer association of liturgy and mystic life and a fuller grasp of the sacrament as a *mysterium*. Unending vistas open on beautiful land, which has so long been barred by hedges and outcroppings sown and then neglected by the men of the Dark Ages, into which later men did not dare penetrate. For hundreds of years we have lived in a self-imposed narrow patch of apologetic theology, watered by a thin trickle coming down to us from the dammed-up lake of individual mysticism, while the distant roar of the pure waters of sacramental, communal, and ecclesial mysticism seemed only to be heard by the saints.

Third: The relationship of the three phases of Christ's Body— historical, sacramental, ecclesial—changed gradually until the time of St. Thomas, whose epigones made it a static and fixed change. But up to the time of the great change, the sacramental body had been associated with the Church; the sacramental and ecclesial body were treated as the most closely related phases. The historical body was in a looser relationship. But, in the fight against Berengar's heresy, writers first, then teachers, then preachers, then mystics and finally the faithful began (and continue to this day) to associate the sacramental Body of Our Lord with his historical Body in the first instance.

That is a tremendous change of emphasis. In order to avoid a mis- understanding, let us say at once that the doctrine of the Church, of course, did not change. What was taught from then on was not new, nor was the old tradition declared wrong or faulty. It was a change of emphasis, caused by a new interest and a new attitude.

Let us illustrate this shift of emphasis. Take a rose. I can de- scribe it as a rich, deep-colored flower of the most delicate scent produced by nature. But I can also say that it is a creeping shrub of the rosaceous genus with five petals and a prickly stem. In both cases, I have a true rose. The first description shows me a live rose in all its beauty; the second classifies the rose botanically.

Thus one can also deal with the Holy Eucharist. Augustine de- scribed it the first way as did the liturgical texts and the Fathers. It became the sacred banquet to be eaten to build up the Church, the living Body of Christ. The bread showed the oneness of the many as the wine did. Each grain of wheat had to be ground to flour and endure the fire's heat to be baked into one bread, just as Christ and his Church became one through his Passion, Crucifixion, and Resurrection. This was the ecclesial Christ who suffered a grinding and fiery pain and whose character has been impressed on our sufferings in the mystery of baptism to make us one with him. Like a family, the grapes for the wine had grown together on the vine; the process they underwent, when trodden out to shed their juice like blood, made them into one and revealed a hidden fiery power until the exhilarating wine was consecrated into the redeeming blood of the Christ. This was the theology of the Fathers and is still the theology of our liturgy—if we have not "mislearned" to read its ancient texts. It is the theology our people need; it builds families into a oneness in Christ, into the parish, into the Church.

But with the second view taken from natural science, you can develop a sort of supernatural botany or chemistry. You will be as right as the Fathers. The question is, Where does this Aristotelian chemistry lead us if it is not balanced by Augustine's whole view? Its road is strewn with the skeletons of those who came to naught on it—Berengar, Wycliffe, Calvin, Hus, Luther, Jansen, and all the little doubters and victims of this approach. Its outcome is individualism. What is left of the wide, complete, and dynamic wholeness of the doctrine? Only one facet of the crystal, the Real Presence of the historical Christ, static and undynamic, provoking, not reactions of conscious, dynamic, and corporate life, but silent worship of the "loving gaze," as Father Joseph Kramp, S.J., called it. The building up of the Body of Christ, known and discussed by scholars, has receded from the mind of the devotional writer, the retreat master, the novice mistress, the teaching nun, and the preacher, and is completely absent in devotional literature. Instead, the historic Christ glorified is reduced to a visitor, promising sweet spiritual intercourse and bridal embraces—a "soul-God" relationship that makes every effort to shut out the outer world. Monads walk up to the altar rail to commune with the divine Monad and walk back hugging their secret for solitary enjoyment of presence. A great confusion of the real loving gaze of eternity, the ecstatic gaze of the true mystic and the gaze on the mere species of the Blessed Sacrament has made our first Communion instruction a tangle of unseen visions, dogmatic deductions of a questionable kind, and unlived sensations of disappointed adepts of mysticism. In seminaries and novitiates these strange growths assume tropic proportion. What can the family do with it? Is their oneness only an intentional, a moral one, like a number of instruments sounding the same note? Or is it not rather an ontological oneness in Christ as the Fathers and Thomas Aquinas saw it?

We seem to have lost the positive aspects of the Holy Eucharist through defensive apologetic ideas. While theology should defend the Real Presence of Our Lord in the reserved Blessed Sacrament, our dwelling on this one aspect has resulted in an attitude that is destructive of a richer Eucharistic life, which goes beyond the relations of the individual soul and the hidden Christ and which would give us back that communal Christ whom the early Fathers preached long before any heretic dared question the reality of our sacraments. We still have to implement the task that Pius X showed us and to refill the vessels of doctrine that are now standing dry or half empty.

If we had nothing to offer our families, our parishes, but the customary motives for corporate Communion we should succeed neither materially nor spiritually. The counting of Communions may satisfy the statistician in us, the reaching of high records may flatter our competitive spirit, the demonstration of faith and obedience may give us moral satisfaction, the family Communion or what is left of it, may have highly educational or pedagogic value, but all these considerations make the center of our life a means to an end that is inferior to it! All of them are individualistic. None of them approaches directly the Body of Christ; none is ecclesial.

It is a strange phenomenon in things as spiritual as theology to see that when apologetics gets hold of something, it follows the irritant, the heresy, a long way and, going out into the desert, it takes a long time to come home. As a tree on the seacoast that is exposed to constant western winds bends eastward and develops its foliage on one side only, so—on the popular level that includes catechism instruction, popular devotions, and parochial and mission oratory—the constant blowing of the evil wind of error has presented us with a strangely impoverished version of Eucharistic life. The decrees of Pius X so far have not straightened the tree, but have merely put more branches and leaves on one side of it. And is it not an old experience that constant winds shake off the fruit before it is ripe?

We live in the twentieth, not in the tenth or sixteenth century. A Catholic who accepts the virgin birth of Our Lord, who bows to the infallibility of the Pope, and all the other dogmas of our Faith has hardly any difficulty in believing Christ's own words: "This is My Body; This is the Chalice of My Blood." Luther's, Calvin's, Wycliffe's and Berengar's different interpretations are by now curious museum pieces. Why fill our schoolbooks with defenses against enemies gone and dead, while the hearts of men hunger and thirst for a new vision of life? Why give nontheologians a *rough* sketch of what is *subtle,* a whiff of academic air that will never be fully breathed by 99 per cent of them. Why load them down with heavy sacks full of the debris from academic studies?

What then are the conclusions we can draw from a fuller grasp of the Holy Eucharist? The mere literal obedience to Communion decrees is not enough; it must be accompanied by a strenuous effort of freeing, as from fetters, the thoughts of generations that slipped into the attitude which the Church so vigorously condemned at the Lateran and Tridentine councils and in St. Pius X. We must revise our preaching by reading Ignatius of Antioch, Augustine, Ambrose, Chrysostom, and by a more literal and accurate acceptance of the texts of our own Roman missal, especially in its Canon and its ancient texts of the true "Proper of the Times." We must broaden by this study the restricted and unilateral influence of later authors, like Thomas à Kempis and others, to greater and more vital richness of doctrine. We must express this new and yet ancient richness in better celebration of the mysteries in every parish church, from the humble low Mass to the solemn Sunday parish Mass. No monads, but members, cells of a Body. Thus we must create the atmosphere our families will breathe and the climate whose sun shines eternally from the Father through the Son and fills His Body with its soul, the Spirit.

3

Lent: Rebirth and Resurrection

LENT IN FOCUS

As have all things instituted by Holy Church, Lent has a history, and a long one. Naturally this history is one of ups and downs, of shifts of emphasis, of struggles between original conceptions and their reflection in the popular mind. Ideas are seldom comprehended in the pure state that they existed in when they were born in the minds of their creators; they lead instead the life that is destined for them as they take their shape: look, for example, at the Constitution and what has happened to the original idea of the electoral college. Even persons, concrete and real as they are, accumulate legends which gradually become almost ineradicable, such as the legend that has grown up about Lincoln. No wonder creations of the spirit suffer permutations; and these changes that ideas undergo in the popular mind, changes which finally succeed in carrying the day over the original version, have, of course, like legends about persons, some kind of foundation.

Let us, for argument's sake, assume the following to be the facts—and there is good reason to believe that this is what really happened: the early Christians were so intensely *living toward* the final return of Jesus in triumph, the present world to them was such a passing thing, that they followed the weekly Sabbath, the end of the week and the symbol of rest in the Old Covenant, with a vigil which was called the "Lord's Day," prefiguring *"the* Day." This observance had a twofold character. Since it followed the seventh day, it naturally was the *eighth day,* which meant, since the

39

natural week has only seven days, that it was, so to speak, a step beyond, out of time into a new "aion," a new kind of era, something like eternity. It was therefore a constant reminder that Christians were waiting, suspended between victory (the Paschal mystery) and triumph (the parousia, the "being present"; as Jesus said, using the present tense, "Before Abraham came to be, *I am.*"). This vigil simply consisted of that one thing Jesus had left His followers on the eve of His departure into the "new aion," when He told them "to do this, keeping memory of Me until I come": the sacred banquet of Bread and Wine, symbolizing and making His separated Body and Blood a sacrifice.

The records show that these vigil services, whose character is still preserved in our Ember Saturdays, in the vigil Masses, and above all in "the Great Night," the supremely beautiful services of the Easter Vigil, were usually held before dawn on Sunday, and afterward the early Christians went to work. And, since this vigil took place on the *first day* of the new week, it also served as a striking symbol of the other, the "Martha," aspect of the Church's mission: to go out to teach and to transform the world. Only later did the Church permit a transfer of the notions of the Old Testament to the New Kingdom, and then she sought for herself Jewish institutions, which were fulfillments of the old prophecies, like a Christian Sabbath.

Scholarly research now seems to confirm that this weekly Pasch preceded the celebration of the annual Pasch. This development probably happened either while the Apostles were still with the Church or soon after. Its seasonal attuning to spring and rebirth helped to make Baptism its central theme, in its ancient and full rite of burial-resurrection. The ceremony of immersion (Baptism by immersion is still practiced in Benevento, Italy, and is provided as an alternate in the latest Roman ritual) seen as resurrection carries with it a prevalently Pauline character. St. John's favorite emphasis on rebirth is expressed in the beautiful images of Paschal poetry still sung on the occasion of the blessing of the baptismal font, as the womb of the Church, fertilized by the Spirit for the rebirth of the New Man, and lends itself equally well to the ancient custom of full immersion.

It is this double character of the *New Man*, the second Adam, Christ, and those mystically incorporated into Him by Baptism, and of parousia, the *coming* of the Lord and our *waiting* for Him, our making ready for both, which formed and fashioned Easter.

The result of these considerations is, then, that Lent, unless we assume that it was an accidental and haphazard conglomeration of things that grew like weeds, is inspired and designed as a preparation for these two mysteries which are the sum of the whole economy of salvation. Since the season was spring and since one can really be baptized only once in his life, two mental adjustments were made: spring brought the newness, the rebirth and resurrection, into clearer focus and, by the time our present standard texts had been chosen for the Latin and Roman liturgy, the concomitant idea of the final triumph had been lifted out and it developed by itself into a second cycle, which seems to start later in the year.

This new cycle opens with the great Ember Vigil in the fall and the Eighteenth Sunday after Pentecost. It finds its "parousial" climax in the three eschatological (from the Greek *ta eschata*, the last things: Christ's return, the Resurrection of all, the triumph of justice in His Judgment, the ensuing Glory) flourishes of the Advent cycle: Christmas, Epiphany, and Candlemas. The removal of one of the component ideas from this season took away some of its original emphasis on the Lord's coming and magnified and enlarged the rebirth and resurrection aspect. Further weight was given to the spring and rebirth aspects by the fact that Lent grew into the period set aside for the immediate preparation for Baptism. It became quite early the baptismal retreat of the Church. If we remember that the exorcisms, and the rendering of the Apostles' Creed and Lord's Prayer by the candidates, the opening of the ears and nostrils for better "*sapere*," spiritual discrimination, and other ceremonies which are now telescoped into one rite that often seems like a legal performance, if we remember that all this was originally spaced with great sagacity, in a natural rhythm over the whole of Lent, then it becomes even more obvious that the task of Lent is the building of the New Adam, the conditioning of all that in man that is to be the soil for spiritual growth.

That this was not only done by an expert in psychology, education, and spiritual discipline, but by a genius with almost "musical" talent, becomes evident when we thumb meditatively through the texts of our Missal, starting with the somber chords of Septuagesima and ending in the glowing and brilliant finale of Whitsunday. There are no discrepancies, no *"non sequiturs"*; there is no piling up instead of growing; you notice no jerking from one attitude into another. All is organic growth with due transition and sensible sequence. There are none of the abrupt and incoherent changes of unguarded tradition, whim, and emotion. The subtle allusions, the overtones, and the ascending and descending climaxes betray the hand of great masters. If such an analysis were proof, one might suspect that a Father like Damasus or Gregory the Great, whose role has so long been dismissed as a pious legend, was the principal architect or composer of this theandric song of redemption.

The other adjustment of our mind is needed because of the simple fact that few of us are really preparing for Baptism; since the "parousial" aspect has largely been moved to the second cycle of the Church year, this annual retreat must be actualized in a new way. It would be the simplest thing in the world to lay the emphasis on an annual rebuilding of the New Man in us, or what the time-worn terminology of our day calls a renewal of Baptism. Not of baptismal vows only, but the fullness of Baptism lived in a participation of mind, heart, and body in the three last days of Holy Week, after six weeks or more of careful, gradual, and complex conditioning, culminating in the "Great Night" of the Easter Vigil. Then the secondary observances like fasting and other taming devices of wild and fallen nature would become natural corollaries, and there could not but result a rebirth and resurrection of the Church and her members each Easter.

As everywhere else, here, too, it is hard for later generations to grasp and maintain the grand sweep of the towering spiritual structure made of the granite blocks of Redemption, ordered and arranged in a composition whose theme and purpose we have outlined, and tightly cemented in majesty and ardor by logic, and by respect for nature and growth and the idea of infinite progression, beaten out by the rhythm of nature.

The ages following the Fathers were analytic, curious, playful, satisfied with the idea that all was already fulfilled. Instead of straining forward collectively, they looked back and chose details from the whole, as one might go home after a symphony humming or whistling themes of impressive tunes without being able to retain the full work. The subordinate things became all-important: the penitential character—without it there is no preparation for God's contemporaneity; the attendance at, more than the sequence of daily Masses, the earnest of withdrawn living, the "pasch-ektomy" or isolation of the physical and psychic suffering of Our Savior; in short, the things one does and those that hurt.

This was accompanied by the great leveling tendency of all popular activities, the drive toward repetition and monotony, the chafing away of the finely chiseled, the wearing away of the subtly rhythmed, the preference for the rudimentary, ordinary, and bulky over the differentiated, well scaled, and proportioned. The devices, the subsidiary and partial aspects gradually rose to such heights that you had to climb high up to see beyond them the distinct outlines of what they had overgrown and put into the shadowy background.

However, it would be totally unrealistic to construe an either-or alternative here. "Popular" is not the same as plebeian and vulgar. Popular piety and devotion are good things as long as they have a rising and elevating tendency in their quality. It is only watered-down and emptied-out mysticism, originally genuine emotion and true sentiment, that becomes cheap emotionalism. Liturgy deteriorated into ritualism and performance may parade as popular devotion, while it is really a debased version of a greater thing. But as steppingstones, popular or, rather, current practices have their place as much as the liturgy, which is a higher form of worship because it is not only more God-centered, but is either itself a sacrament instituted by the Lord and containing Him, or an unfolding of such sacraments, just as Lent unfolds the total content of Baptism and the Eucharist.

Sacraments and their organic, essential developments, called liturgy, are means to an end: to worship and to attain the infinite God. Popular devotions, often deriving from the liturgy or its coarser imitation, but more often less sublime results of man's groping and striving, are also steppingstones. However, in our celebration of Lent, above all other seasons the greatest and richest of the Church's spiritual year, these Masses, these texts of the breviary, are the most important, whatever our parish churches may offer.

The daily station Mass, with its constant and changing wealth of God's Word, is more important than the customary devotions, though we should never neglect them in the name of the liturgy. It would be the kiss of death for the liturgical movement if we formed esoteric conventicles of the elect and the highbrow, disrupting the parish, in the name of the Church "non-existent." *Mediator Dei* has been called the encyclical that establishes equilibrium in the Mystical Body and, while it rebukes the imprudent, it also severely scolds those who are lethargic, ignorant, and stubborn. The sooner lay people use intelligently and in greater numbers the books of the Church, not mechanically thumbing through them, but as guide and inspiration in their approach to God through His Mediator, the earlier the existing gaps between altar and nave, clergy and laity, popular devotion and sacred liturgy, subjective emotionalism and God's revelation, will be closed.

The practical difficulty of finding a church where the Mass "of the day," the actual Lenten Mass will be said, can be solved by requesting the Mass of the day when an offering is made. If groups of people get together, in parish after parish, to do this, there will soon be hardly a parish which does not avail itself of this great privilege expressly granted by the Pope Saint Pius X for this purpose.

Not only Rome, but Venice, Milan, Paris, Linz and Vienna have revived the station Masses. One church, or chapel, is officially appointed every day in Lent to represent the station in Rome. The bishop and clergy gather at this church and thousands of the laity come to it to make their station every day. In France, Germany, and Austria, where evening Masses are now common, this is especially easy to do. There is no reason in the world why Catholics in our great cities cannot, privately or in groups, do the same. The Church knows that drabness, monotony, and restriction to mental prayer only are mistakes, creating, as they do, a reaction of blind emotionalism, since they split the living man in two. The full and healthy man cries for color, signs, and symbols as he cried for the living Word made flesh in Jesus.

THE SPIRIT OF LENT

Even a superficial look at Lenten usages discloses a discrepancy between those observed in our parishes and those of the Roman missal. The popular observance of Lent is narrowly concentrated on the Passion of Our Lord. Neither the priest's daily prayer book, his breviary, nor the missal follows this pattern.

To the average Catholic the season is a series of negative rules: don't smoke, don't drink, don't eat enough, don't dance, don't go to shows, don't get as much sleep in the morning because you go to Mass. It all starts out with ashes on a gray morning after a last fling, and the priest's words, "Remember that thou art dust and that to dust thou wilt return," sound a somber note as an overture to forty days' severity.

The "athletic" aspect, if it may be called so, prevails. Add to this the mite box full of dimes and pennies, the daily attendance at Mass, the sermons on moral reform, the Stations of the Cross, and the crowning of it all by the Easter reception of the Sacrament of Penance, and you have a sketch of the hard and fixed tradition in our parishes up and down the land. There is no doubt that the current customs produce salutary results, that the clergy are accustomed to running their parishes in this fashion and that, without a suspicion that there could be an alternative; the people take it for granted that this is the way Lent goes and has gone for hundreds, maybe thousands of years.

One might assume that the large number of people who use a missal at Mass might feel a bit uneasy. I am not talking about the aesthetic malaise of the mental ear that hears instruments playing, so to speak, that are out of tune. This is definitely not a question of aesthetics. It is emphatically a profoundly spiritual question. With the help of a little bit of history, we can see this easily, because when one sees how a thing grew one suddenly understands.

First let it be clear that we are not talking about an unrealistic Utopia. What the documents of the Church offer is so dazzling, so spiritual, and presumes such a deep, mature, and assimilated faith, that we neither hope to see a change in one generation nor expect the present customs to be entirely absorbed into the liturgical vision of Lent. Priests are not ready for a start in this direction, and the laity has now hardly a way to influence their clergy. The tendency is toward the massive, not the subtle; toward the visible, not the invisible; toward the secondary, not the primary, facts of redemption; toward gloom rather than triumph.

We do not live in a conservative age, and so things may move faster, but we should not forget that the losses of the Reformation left the Church with an outsized majority of static people and deprived her of natural forces that are now badly needed. To become operative, grace is required not only in individuals but also in collectives like parishes and dioceses. And who says that what applies to integral parts does not apply to the whole body? As long as the average Catholic of our day is not disposed to accept St. Pius X's and Pius XII's vision of reform, no decrees and fond dreams of reformers—in the good sense of the word, not the rebellious—will have any effect.

How our present Lent, as it appears officially, came about is easier to understand when we remember that its development came to a halt before the time of Charlemagne; in other words that it greatly changed and grew between about A.D. 250 and 750, but that for the last twelve hundred years it has been unaltered, kept, so to speak, in a deep-freeze. The result is that now we have two Lents, a beautiful "antique" and a rather shoddy-looking thing, our popular version. The word "shoddy" is certainly an objectionable term for which I may be taken to task, but it is meant comparatively.

Before the first change the whole complex of redemption was liturgically celebrated in one service, the Great Night; there was no Palm Sunday, no Maundy Thursday, or Good Friday. In their sacramental worship Christians did not look back (in meditation and instruction they did, of course), but forward with a fixed gaze toward the second coming.

We do not exactly know when the distribution of the different phases of Redemption started. The Feast of the Ascension, for example, was an established feast by A.D. 339; Epiphany and Christmas are a little older. Holy Week seems to be the result of the influx of pilgrims into the Holy Land and their subsequent interest in the memorable places and then, naturally, the memorable days. The short one-day fast grew gradually into its present length in the seventh century. At about the same time the three pre-Lenten Sundays were introduced. The primary purpose of the long fast with a daily afternoon Mass, except on Thursdays, was the preparation of the catechumens for Baptism; this purpose, not the Passion of Our Lord or the annual penance of the already baptized, is what we notice in the choice of the texts.

The most helpful attitude an adult and mature Christian can adopt in order to benefit spiritually from the treasure heaped up in the missal is to take stock of what is there and what is not there. But note that this is no invitation to sabotage the "popular" parochial Lenten observances and to form esoteric conventicles of "the spiritual betters" as nuclei of resistance against hard-working pastors. The saints were individuals who did all that the people did, but who saw more and had richer resources. The penitential element in Lent is as necessary as the rest of things.

Lent by itself is incomplete. The cycle begins with Septuagesima Sunday and ends with Pentecost. Its climax is the Easter Vigil, naturally, in its conjunction with Good Friday and the following paschal tide. ("Tide" is a good word for the tidal wave of joy that it stands for.) Except for the Friday Masses which contain hints and subtle allusions, the liturgy does not mention the Passion until the Monday before Passion Sunday, when St. John's Gospel takes over and presents the growing conflict between Jesus and His adversaries. This struggle becomes more and more explicit and reveals above all the mental and spiritual agony—*agon strife*—of the Savior and draws us all into this crisis. There is progression and transition, as against the repetition and abruptness in our popular practices and customs. While there are traces of meddling and importation from the outside, even the existing missal texts show a sweep toward a climax that provides almost a musical pleasure, to step for a moment into the realm of aesthetics.

One factor easily forgotten is the fact that our missal is definitely the common book of sacraments of the city of Rome and was not originally composed for the Church Universal. The whole Church is seen as an appendix of the city of Peter: the Masses are all assigned to definite church buildings in Rome and some of them are so parochial in their texts that a text was chosen to fit the mosaics in the apse of that church. This will delight some who love and know Rome and have an ultramontane bent; it will annoy others who have a hard time in seeing consistency in the choice of texts. With a humble heart, all of us should be able to make an adjustment and, a good introduction in hand, gather spiritually in that church, called the "station church." The fare of scripture is so rich, the facets in which we "see Jesus" day after day so varying that we need not be upset by the localization of the texts.

A word of warning is needed. Even if we know this background, the propers of the Lenten Masses which season the unchanging fare of the ordinary are mutilated. The Introits have only one psalm verse and often not the significant one. There is only one third left of the

Offertory verse, and often the amputation has removed the heart. The Communion antiphon (*"communio"*) is a frame without a picture because the psalm is missing, and the psalm, to be sung congregationally while all receive Holy Communion, is very often what links Communion with the Gospel and the other parts of the Mass.

A good program for spiritual reading in this Lenten period would therefore be to read the missing parts on the eve of, or before, Mass, so that every Mass makes the full impact on the participant it originally was meant to make. As long as the reform of the missal is a fond hope, we have to do the best we can with what we have. The Austrians were more fortunate than we because Father Pius Parsch actually printed complete and restored missals for Lent for the use of the laity. Once you have tried this rich repast, the sense of loss when you hold the truncated missal in your hands is so tremendous that you will never rest in prayer and effort until a remedy is provided.

Some people may think this is all most irregular. But see what has happened: had there been no clamor from the crowd there would not have been Pius X's reforms. And, alas, the sketchy implementation of his decrees shows that the clamor was neither loud nor persistent enough. Look at some of the things Pope Pius XII did: evening Mass, vernacular rituals, the Easter Vigil, and a real hope of a popular form of the Mass kindled and maintained! These were things asked for, begged for, even after the first applicants were turned down and poorly instructed voices called "heresy and schism!"

To return to the subject at hand, we must readjust our conception of Lent to get its true benefits. First we must see it is part of a whole. We must realize that we should take the hand of the Church to be led above the level of current substitutions. We must keep in mind that, in spite of mutilations, it is a carefully and artfully contrived entity with a direction and meaning. We must see that its meaning is positive, that its penitential aspects are means to an end and should make for a greater inflowing of grace and a deeper conception of our redeemed estate. We must consciously see in Lent a rebirth, as is suggested by the original purpose of preparation for Baptism, now made very real through the Easter "duties" and the renewal of Baptism *in voto* during the Sacred Night. We must also cultivate, and do so consciously, the spirit of the fifty days following the Sacred Night in which we learn to walk on this higher level of the "Eighth Day," in a new aion, eternity anticipated.

All of Lent's auxiliary observances of penance and purification should ever be performed with a deep conviction that purification is God's work and all our works are His gifts, thus avoiding semi-Pelagian pride. Lent should be an annual "crisis," a rebirth in the spirit, and all the "athletics" of hardships we impose on ourselves are vain unless we also expose our minds and hearts to the Word and to the Sacrament. This is the meaning of the gentle sequence of the missal, its subtle timing, its steady urging and pleading.

Someone long ago remarked that this method is too diffuse for modern men and women, that it is better achieved by such means as truly Ignatian retreats, for example, or heart-piercing missions. Liturgical extremists, on the other hand, have belittled these means as too violent, as momentary flashes in the pan.

But surely we need not oppose one way to another. St. Ignatius was gentler because he distributed his "crisis" over thirty days, not three, and our three and ten-day retreats are really preparations for an annual stocktaking. As a sacramental Church, incarnational as she is, the Christian Church of Catholic tradition must regain in a body and in a common annual experience what she loses in apostolic salt in the frittering away of everyday life. Modern man needs the sledgehammer blows to break the crust of secularism, but the gentle effort made "in the world" by parishes as a whole during Lent is as modern as a "secular institute."

I, for one, think with a great number of priests and laymen that the full wealth locked up in Latin and clerical ritualism must be unlocked and spread by a reform coming from the proper authorities, and I would fear for our youth's faith if halfway measures and grudging concessions, too little and too late, were the outcome of our clamor for bread. The record of what has been achieved, however, stands, and the present wave of pessimism is but a test of our courage, humility, and patience. It is sad that a great deal of intellectual equipment is as yet needed to get a fuller experience of Lent. Yet the fact cannot be denied. But those who can do so should; they should not be satisfied with substitutes. This can be done without loss either of humility or of a sense of community with those who are deprived of this wealth. To quote an inept example from another field: you may thoroughly savor Berlioz' *L'enfance du Christ* and yet be charmed by a simple Christmas carol.

The unsolved problem of our great liturgy, especially that of Lent-Pentecost, is a burden to be picked up by those who strive after a mature Christianity. Even though few of us will be given the gift of supernaturally founded elation at Easter, able to sing the Introits, Alleluias, Offertories, and Communions—with their psalms!—in our hearts with no residuum of unrealized, tardy sloth, all of us will gain a nearness to Christ's Mystical Body, a comprehension of salvation, an integration into the stream of pneumatic tradition which is rarely given by the substitutes for the "Word and Sacramental mystery" (liturgy), and then more by a leap across them than by them.

The great theme is sounded on the first Sunday in Lent, after four days of preparation, in the Gospel of Christ's temptation. All through Lent the psalm of this Sunday, so closely joined to the Gospel, is repeated. Thus Lent is not routine; it is a time of decision, of plowing the hard surface of habit, of seeding the Word into the furrows made by penance, of forming heart and mind according to the foreshadowing in the Old and the reality in the New Testament, woven into the superb pattern of the missal. The labor and penance, the renunciation of the alluring evil, striven after with more or less energy and success, will become a deep religious experience in its full sense only if we follow the Church in her liturgy—because Word and Sacrament are the only immediately given means of salvation for those who aspire to Faith and Love.

THE REFORMED LENTEN LITURGY

All of Lent is a preparation for Holy Week. It seems, however, as if few Catholics realize how subtle a preparation, how gradual a progress and how "direction-wise" a preparation this is. There is a definite one-way movement toward Easter in the day-after-day progress of the Masses and the prayers. As the scenes of a play are strung together, each begetting the next and progressing toward the climax, so day follows day, week begets week in this dramatic building up of thought, emotion, and will power to the fullness of the Holy Triduum or Threeday. As Holy Week was made new by recent reforms so Lent, as yet in a minor key, must be made new. The old preparation won't do for the new or rather renewed observance.

Before we go any further, let us make sure we are not misunderstood: we are talking about the liturgy of Lent only, that is, the Mass and the prayers that arc said in the breviary, and even there we have no intention of anticipating any reforms, as they say, "*ad mentem sanctae sedis,*" in the general direction in which the Holy See is going in its reforms: the texts and the ceremonies will be the same for all whether they are in accordance with the spirit of the new decrees or ignore them. The first job is to find out what principles governed the reforms of Holy Week and how many of them can be applied to our keeping of Lent. This naturally will show also how far we can go without breaking the forms that exist, and where we must stop. It will therefore mainly be a job of refocusing existing practices.

The restoration of Holy Week seems to have been governed by the following considerations: (1) to clear away those features that obstruct the view of the essentials and to bring out these essentials with greater clarity: (2) to remake the rites so that the people can not only understand them better, but above all are naturally drawn into them by participating in them in taking their part opposite the clergy and the singers: (3) to make clear beyond doubt by its very performance that we deal not only with the heart of the liturgical Church year, but of salvation: it is an unfolding in rite and sacrament of the whole content of our Redemption, and its climax is the Resurrection-Baptism resulting from the Passion of Our Lord into which we as the Church are merged. Lent harnesses our nature for this sacramental work, gradually guides our thoughts and nurses our emotions into a state where we can best become a part of this sacred liturgy. Through the fact that it is sacrament it is true presence and reality; not in a historical and naturalistic way, nor by the pure meditation and emotional effort of the celebrating subject; it is a reality all its own, carefully called sacramental, but it is a reality.

Without cutting out any of our customary Lenten practices, even the least essential or incongruent ones, let us see what we can do to separate in our minds the essential features from the possible obstructions. The reform I have in mind is, therefore, one of attitudes: habits of thinking and acting, not of rubrics and texts. The first requirement then for a renewed Lent is that we consider it as a preparation for Easter and observe it consistently as that. Of course, in a vague way it has always been one, but all the practices point out that the progression in Lent was not fully realized in popular customs. Lent began on Ash Wednesday, and the preceding three Sundays, which should have conditioned us for this solemn opening of a sacred journey, were either ignored or at best "honorably mentioned" as pre-Lenten period.

To make the point clearer, let us borrow an image from music: on Ash Wednesday a chord was struck, four notes, (1) fasting, (2) no amusement, (3) Stations of the Cross, (4) special sermons on some important subject. This chord was held, sounded all through Lent, and then at the end there was the glorious melody of Easter, when the monotonous chord stopped, either on the sacred Threeday or on Saturday afternoon with the Easter confession. This is something to remember: It was the same sound all through Lent, and it was not—and this is important to know—played from the official score or printed music provided by the Church in the missal, the breviary, and other liturgical books. This score would have provided variations, a sustained crescendo, movements and themes. But these musical variations were never heard by the people because the customary "Lent" developed in the ages of the "Latin-wall between the altar and the pew" when the laity were regarded as too simple, too inert, and too immature to be introduced to such a rich score. And this attitude boomeranged on the clergy: they too attuned themselves to the monotony of the four-note chord; they may have added a fifth tone or even a sixth and they may have made it sound a bit stronger than the laity's chord, but on the whole they finally followed the people's way of keeping Lent. Of course, they read the score with their lips forming sonorous Latin words, but their hearts were really warmed by the sound of that "chord," not by the rich score.

We would frustrate a great deal of the newly unlocked treasures of the Holy Week, with their great possibilities for popular participation and with their clear outline of essentials versus nonessentials, if we obstinately persisted in not adapting Lent to its refurbished goal and aim. Let us see, then, what the liturgical *symphony*, as opposed to the one-chord *monotony*, has to offer and, with the laity in mind, let us take stock only of the missal.

The missal sets forth the season of Lent in stages and by degrees. To enter into this gradual initiation, into the mystery of rebirth and Resurrection which is the content of the Threeday from Good Friday to Easter—the Pasch—and to reform ourselves in an *annual Baptism*, we have to go through these stages. There is first the pre-Lenten period, the Sundays Septuagesima until Ash Wednesday: they are not only beautifully chosen in their readings and song texts, but they are also summaries of the whole spirit of Lent. I shall let my readers explore their own missals, from the call to watchful earnestness on the first Sunday to the high canticle of love on the last of them. If you have "done" them with the Church, reading or listening with an eager heart, you are ready for the second stage. You hear the call to conversion, fasting, and penance on Ash Wednesday in the church of St. Sabina; to prayer on Thursday at St.

George's Roman shrine, the church that was once Cardinal New-man's; and to good works, and almsgiving on Friday at the Church of Sts. John and Paul, the martyrs whose Lent was bloodshed for their faith: perfect charity.

Not only does the Church gather you daily at Mass, but she calls you in spirit into one of the ancient Roman *title churches* making thus the round of the sacred city. Learned writers like H. Grisar or Cardinal Schuster have investigated the connection between the choice of the texts chosen for the individual Masses and the church in which the Mass takes place and came up with astonishing rela-tions between the two. They explain much that was otherwise obscure. But for our purposes we have enough to do to refocus Lent without such intricacies, as long as we remember that even this list of churches adds to the variety in the spiritual Lenten fare, and as long as we make a mental note to be with the Roman cate-chumens for whose benefit this was all made available.

These stages were originally stages for converts to the faith who went through a forty-day intensive training period to die and rise with Christ on the Sacred Threeday. It is important, not just interest-ing and enlightening, to know this. The Church has kept this pattern of seriousness and of dedication that we find in all real conversions and asks us to go through this conversion every spring and to die to ourselves and live for Christ on the Sacred Threeday. This is so formidable a task that the Church does not expect us to comprehend its fullness in one sermon or a few lessons, but by being led from stage to stage, from daily Mass to daily Mass, step by step, fed in small spoonfuls and with varied flavor added at each Mass. As a symphony reveals its beauty and unity of conception from theme to theme and movement to movement to the final triumphant bar, so Lent leads us through the degrees of spiritual initiation to the final bar: the Great Night when we experience our own incorpora-tion in the risen Christ by Baptism (renewal of vows) and Com-munion.

The next stage is Lent proper, because until the first Sunday all has been preliminary to it and after Laetare Sunday Passiontide begins. And again here we find groupings of great beauty and wisdom: there are the three Ember Day Masses: Elias, Ezechiel, and Moses loom up with their great visions calling us to contemplation and transfiguration through the sacraments of the New Covenant. There are the Thursday Masses with their practical exhortations. There are the Fridays with their miracles of foreboding that carry in the womb of mystery the tragedy of the Jews on Good Friday, those miracles that angered the Pharisees and persons in authority in Jerusalem most of all. On these Fridays we feel drawn to the Master in his distress, his courage and his messianic loneliness. The more emotional "first" Friday finds here its more soteriological (from the Greek Soter tou Kosmou—Redeemer of the Universe) prototype steeped in sacred history and set into the framework of Redemption. There is another group: from the Saturday before the second Sunday until the following Wednesday the Masses vary the theme of the sinner and the merciful God in their gospels. Or you may want to group this same Saturday with the following one and call them Saturdays of Mercy, as one tells of the prodigal son and the other of the woman caught in adultery. Laetare Sunday is a joyful breather: the Cross is hailed in its main sanctuary in Rome, and the Holy Eucharist is foreshadowed in the multiplication of bread, to be followed by the advance messengers of Passiontide: the "strife-gospels" from Monday on, almost all of them during the next two weeks taken from St. John.

Thus we have entered imperceptibly the time of the anguish of soul and Passion of Christ which mount steadily to their height on Good Friday. Meditating with the help of the other texts of the Masses and the prophetic lessons of the Old Testament, we go into the soul of Christ, deeper than Stations can lead us and with more varied love of the mind and heart. The Saturday and the *Great* Wednesday in this week preceding the First Passion Sunday are full of hints that it was a week for immediate preparation of the catechumens. The Wednesday gospel—the healing of the man born blind and his valiant witness to Jesus—rivals the fatal Friday gospel in decisiveness in calling us to allegiance renewed in these prototypes.

We cannot even try to set this all into the sparkling mosaic of chant texts, collects, and epistles and to weave the threads of interrelationship and significance between all of them. The Christian taking the hand of the Church in the missal will discover this world of truth and beauty in untiring meditation of the sacred reading and singing.

This firm motherly hand has gently and gradually drawn us into the Passiontide and depth of the soul of Jesus suffering. As in real life there are ups and downs, depths and heights, fright and confidence in an extricable web. We are borne toward the Great Week whose shadow is cast before it in the symbolism of this time: the veils over statues and images, the silence of all joy.

It is a joy to apply the spirit of the already accomplished restoration to the rest of Lent. We have been taught the method by the principles Rome applied to Holy Week; to participate, to look first at essentials, and to view the liturgy as part of our Faith and life. If we try and try again every year in unending patience to plow and seed and harrow our souls in the spring (whose old English translation spells Lent), it will sprout and blossom and bear fruit until the soil is so much improved and our skill so developed that grace roots deeply in our nature.

4

The Christmas Cycle

CHRISTMAS CURRENTS

In the stream of our Christmas consciousness there are visible currents that never seem to mix. I have seen great rivers merge in the same wide bed, one brown and muddy, the other green and crystal clear, and I saw them flow side by side without mingling until I lost sight of the river. This seems to be the case with our ideas of Christmas. There is first the current of the Christmas feast as a bonanza to merchants. It begins with "jingle bells" in October, street lighting in November, carols at any time after Thanksgiving, the red-nosed reindeer in December, and good old jolly potbellied Santa Claus—Wodan-Thor—on Christ's Birthday.

Then there is in the same river bed the current of the Christmas of cribs, Advent wreaths, premature carol singing, wrapped gifts, confession and Holy Communion at Midnight Mass, violin solo, shepherd music, and all that. This current flows side by side with that of the merchants in the river bed of man's mind and emotions. Its best products are baskets of food for the poor and the invitation to a turkey dinner for the lonely.

Then there is the cool and limpid current that runs beneath the others—the liturgy, where Christ-Mass and Epiphany assume imperial and purple color. It is the place of paradox—in the colloquial sense of the word—where such grandiose realities as the first chapters of John and Hebrews, Isaias 60, and the royal Psalm 71 are matched with the narrative of Jesus' birth and the gentle tone of St. Paul's letter to Titus. The very composition of texts and their selection shows a gift for majesty and grandeur. And this is set against the background of Christ's final triumph in his Second Coming, the great Advent of the Lord, his "Presence—parousia."

I have no doubt which of these three currents is the most authentic, comprehensive, and real. Its very subtlety and majesty are the reasons for its submersion by the other currents, even though it gives its name to the great river of Nativity. It will always be difficult for the "masses" of Catholics to comprehend the complex and subtle meaning of the Christmas liturgy and to assimilate it. As a matter of fact, its fate of submersion and oblivion so shortly after it was established is proof that not even the spiritually minded, especially the mystically devout, ever really understood it. The second current, centering on the crib, is the one that has appealed to them, and, in its grosser form, to the ordinary faithful. Yet we should do our best to preserve the liturgical current and to hand it on to future generations, never tiring in our efforts to spread its earnestness and its reality in opposition to the more sentimental, dreamy moods in which we ordinarily find ourselves facing the feast of the Nativity.

While the mystically-minded devout relish the feelings of sympathy with the divine Babe shivering in his crib and barely warmed by the warm animal breath of the legendary ox and ass, the undercurrent, the bass motif, of the coming and Presence should make the Feast of the Nativity a feast of soul searching. For the great earnestness of Christmas is not only in the second coming, in the call for repentance by John the Baptist and Isaias through Advent, but also in the meaning of the stable outside Bethlehem. The past historical event is kerygma, "a message to contemporaries," if we would but listen; kerygma is a word to the heart of man in his present historical situation.

Our historical situation is one of great embarrassment for Christendom. Not only are we stubbornly and scandalously divided among ourselves, but we are mercilessly and coldly sitting at the banquet table while outside our comfortable house Lazarus lies, covered with sores, and hungry. To tell him, in the shape of the Negro, the Andes Indian, the South African miner, the Moroccan, and the "disinherited" that the story ends with Dives in hell and Lazarus in Abraham's bosom is no help to Dives, who happens to be the follower of Christ in this case.

The poor Jesus was born in a stable lent to His parents or occupied by them in their distress without the owner's permission. But now the Christian is in the place once occupied by pagan Romans and easygoing Sadducees. What was once the religion of poverty and renunciation has, according to the penetrating analysis of our own sociologists, become the dynamic power that drives progress forward. Has not a complex chemistry of abortive Judeo-Christian thought, through the failure and blindness of believers, spawned Marxian messianism, with its "sacral" totalitarian empire of a freak social justice, over that part of the globe where social and political injustice had been most rife? While we are fascinated in horror by the cruelty of communism, its disregard of the individual's rights, its atheism, we forget that its success is due to our own callousness and complacency.

This Child in the crib is the Prince of Peace, and angels sing of peace at His birth. The poor next door get a basket of food and some extra fuel to ease our consciences. But are we Christians, Catholics as well as Protestants, perturbed to the degree we should be at the sight of so many who share the Babe's "thrown-ness" into the cruel, insensitive world composed of images of the Creator?

As long as we state all this in general terms, those who do not simply brush such considerations aside as being "un-Christmas-like" will agree, and say how true it all is. But if we become more specific, won't we become controversial? What happened to the moving appeal made by the Boston *Pilot* for expiation of the harm done to Hiroshima, Nagasaki, and Dresden? Archbishop Rummel and the South African hierarchy set wonderful examples in the fight against racism. But where was the popular response? Have Catholics as a whole in certain cities of the North fought for slum clearance? Have Catholics of the West been in the forefront of those who fight for the rights and fair treatment of migratory, seasonal farm laborers? Has there been a wave of Christian revulsion against callous employers who send checks to churches on Sundays, and employ "wetbacks" at fifteen cents an hour during the week, with the collusion of the responsible government agencies?

We have had pointed out to us again and again that the sword of Damocles hangs over the head of the white man on both sides of the iron curtain. The high standard of living protected by power wherever the white man prevails is ineradicably opposed to the abominable conditions of the Andes Indian, the South African miner, the Egyptian fellah, and the masses of India and Indonesia, to mention only those closest to our interest. If the danger hardly makes an impression on us, if our government has to side with its colonizing allies to protect our breadbasket, our shiny cars and TV sets and all that they imply, what chance has the gesture of Almighty God, lying naked in an animal's crib as a little Jewish Babe born of a poor maiden? We shall sing about His birth and what it meant for our sins. We shall thank Him for His love of our unworthiness. But shall we become restless at the thought that He represents those who do not share our "living standard," that His spectacular poverty, which moves pious souls to commiserate with Him, has a worldwide significance? And will we Catholics realize that all eyes are on us?

When we take away from Christmas the silken vestments, the regal passages of Scripture, the magnificence of the cathedrals, the music of incomparable beauty, what remains? God speaking His Word Incarnate as a poor and helpless Infant, the plain bread and wine of His Memorial, the Eucharist. With the wealthy trappings taken away, the Word in Its bareness pierces the soul: "For the Word which God speaks is living and effective and sharper than any two-edged sword. It penetrates to the division of soul and spirit, of joints and marrow, and discerns the thoughts and intentions of the heart. And no creature is hidden from Him: all things are laid bare and are uncovered to the eyes of Him to Whom we have to render account" (Heb. 4:12,13).

Because we have been tardy listeners to the Word, the enemy has seized the cause of the downtrodden and receives credit for his leadership—wrongly perhaps—by those who hunger for bread as well as for justice. Christmas can either be soporific, lulling us in idyllic complacency and complete religious egocentrism, or it can speak the "Thunder-Word" of Bethlehem in its stark reality. Looking into the eyes of the Infant, we meet the direct gaze of all the poor, of those in our own slums and in the depressed areas of the world who hunger after justice.

INCARNATION AND PAROUSIA

If we want to understand the twin feasts of Christmas and Epiphany in their true liturgical meaning, we have to unlearn and to explore a great many commonly accepted things. We should be most willing to do so if we don't want our liturgy to be just a beautiful relic or some ossified pomp without connection with twentieth century life. The winter cycle of the Christian year is a very complex one and has become strange territory to the minds of most of us.

First of all, let us remember that the Church year has two cycles and not three, at least not in the liturgy of our missal and breviary. These two can be most aptly described as the first or Paschal cycle, and the second, or Advent cycle. Sounds a bit startling, doesn't it? But we shall see that the shock which toppled the accepted edifice of our notions about the liturgical year was a sort of slum clearance of our minds: a beautiful old building appears after the incongruous and somehow unsightly obstructions have fallen.

Next, let us, for the time being at least, forget our accepted notion that New Year's Day is anything more than a civic event. Liturgically it is certainly neither the end of anything, except the octave of Christmas, nor the beginning of anything at all. Our New Year's Eve devotions are a concession to modern minds, but they have no bearing whatever on the liturgical development of the Church year. Now, don't be a liturgical fanatic. Don't boycott them, because it would sadden your pastor and your friends. Just give them the right place in your mind, as important for your civic life, your parish, but irrelevant for the liturgical understanding of the Advent or second cycle of the Church year.

Worse than this is my second appeal: forget also for the time being even the idea that the first Sunday in Advent is the beginning of something basically new. I assume that my readers have already cast out of their minds the idea that the four Sundays of Advent symbolize the "four thousand" years before Christ. That idea should have been forgotten long ago. In Milan they have six Advent Sundays, in the Eastern Church something entirely different. Even in our Roman liturgy there have been periods of five and six Advent Sundays. The number is only incidental, and the idea of the "four thousand" years does not fit into a liturgical understanding, which is, after all, what we need now. The first Sunday in Advent is not a caesura, as if there were a deep gap between the last Sunday after Pentecost and the first Sunday of Advent.

The word Advent, *Adventus,* refers to the whole season that has its climax in the Feast of the Epiphany or Theophany. But does this not lessen the status of our beloved Christmas day? Well, if it does, don't accuse the writer. It is liturgical law that the rank of January 6th is higher than that of December 25th, and this is not just stickling, for we shall see later that there is a profound reason for it, even if people nowadays ignore it. (In Rome *Befana* has kept its old rank beside or above *Natale,* Christmas.)

I suppose my readers are eager to know when this season of Advent begins in the liturgical books and when it ends, always remembering that this *Adventus* is a larger unit than what we now call Advent.

If you are expecting something abrupt, you will be disappointed. The Roman liturgy is never abrupt, theatrical, bombastic, and if occasionally one gets such an impression, then something is wrong. Just as night and day flow gently into one another, and as the four seasons develop imperceptibly, the liturgy is something live, growing and organic. There is never anything frantic, hasty, theatrical in the liturgy. The Roman spirit is one of virile moderation and majesty. It was this Roman spirit that made the liturgy. The Kingdom of God is like a mustard seed, like a leaven, and never like a thunderbolt or an earthquake.

In mid-September we have a group of holy days that suggest harvest; the ember days and the triumphal feast of the Holy Cross (September 14th). Around these sacred harvest celebrations, when the leaves begin to turn, we also have the eighteenth Sunday after Pentecost. Through its psalms and lessons and prayers there sounds a faint tinkle of Christmas bells that grow more distinct as the Sundays advance. All Saints and All Souls again strike the note of harvest, but even more, they let us glimpse through the half-open gate into the eternal glory of heaven. That is one of the leading motifs of this great season.

Like the mighty brass mellowed by sweet violins of hope and consolation, the last Sunday after Pentecost and the first Sunday of Advent reveal the grandiose theme of the vision of Christ's return, his parousia: the first, in its terror to Satan and stubborn sinners; the second, with the silver tinge of hope: "Lift up your heads, because the time of your salvation is nigh."

The orchestra of psalms and hymns, of lessons and prayers, never drops these themes: eternity, glory, and parousia. The composer of this celestial symphony then adds two more instruments: the voice of John the Baptist, strong and austere, and of Our Lady, humble, virginal, and pure. It is a constant crescendo from the faint pianissimo of the early fall toward the majestic, fulfilled sound of the parousia motif on Christmas and Epiphany, sounding in its last powerful accord on the second day of February, forty days after Christmas, the beautiful feast of Candlemas.

Here again the last notes of the Advent theme are blended with the first inkling of the new Paschal cycle which sends out its first messengers on Septuagesima Sunday. The arch of this season spans the interval from the eighteenth Sunday after Pentecost to the last Sunday after Epiphany, from Holy Cross to Candlemas.

The grandiose sweep of this liturgical architecture of themes and motifs is visible only after its central theme and mood have been unearthed from medieval and later debris. "What men have done to Christmas!" one could exclaim, if he compared the present vision of this cycle, riveted on the foreground alone, with what he finds in the liturgical books. What have men done? They have taken only partial glimpses of this rich fullness, as if the majestic aspects were too overwhelming, until only disconnected, isolated feasts were visible. When you look on a gigantic chain of snow-capped mountains you see how they belong together. The same chain submerged under a deep ocean shows only disconnected small islands above the surface. You have to let the water recede, as after the great flood, to understand the whole structure.

The idyllic, emotional, affective attitude of the late Middle Ages created this flood of submerging forgetfulness and ignorance. Religion as a commodity of life, as an escape—Marx would say "a drug" —has encouraged this attitude in the bourgeois age. We seem to want the nice little things that smooth the edges of life, not that dynamic, fiery power which purified the Roman Empire and burned out all the straw and wood from its edifice until nothing but the true gold remained to become the temporal shell of Christ's Body, the Holy Roman Church. No wonder this view will at first appear as a frightening vision of eternal values, naked, challenging: *mysterium tremendum.*

Now, should we go and burn all our beautiful hand-carved cribs, our cozy Christmas trees, our sweet Christmas cards with warm, sweet babes in stables, ox and ass included? Are all our naïve shepherd songs to go, the three wise men, the woolly, white poetry of our Nordic winter solstice? Even if our forefathers, those stern men like Leo, Gregory, Ambrose, Augustine, and Damasus, those great poets, such as Sedulius, Venantius, and their companions, composed this wonderful drama, are we, the refined, gentle, or bourgeois men and women of a dying era, made to see their sober, grand architecture? We don't build basilicas with mosaics and Romanesque minsters. Our churches have a drawing-room atmosphere, respectable, full of holy knickknacks and comfortable things. So why should we live intellectually and spiritually on mountaintops of sublime spirituality?

The answer? *"Qui bene distinguit, bene docet"*: of course; nobody advocates throwing present practices into the ash can. I don't know if the present general attitude toward the Advent cycle is healthy and as thoroughly Catholic as it should be. A generation whose whole being does not clamor after final resurrection seems to have lost practical faith in it; its creed is at best a docile recitation. If that generation has no objections to our unjust world and does not cry continually in its soul, with tears of despair, after a better world in which justice is king—*"Ecce advenit dominator Dominus"* (Introit of Epiphany)—then there is some suspicion that its Christians no longer hunger and thirst after justice but are a lot of smug people, whose life is a pretty picture of comfort, framed with the gilt edge of a partial religion.

But we can keep all our modern, beloved Christmas trappings, as long as we see through them and as long as we know that there is a reality and a future behind those things of the past. When we celebrate Midnight Mass in Bethlehem "at the crib," as the missal says; when we go as good pilgrims to the Mass "at dawn" in the Church of the *Anastasis* (Resurrection); and when we see the full glory of the Divine Child in the third Mass, we have already made a seven-league step from the crib idyll toward the full meaning of the parousia. The first coming of the Word is the transparent stained glass through which shine the refracted rays of His final triumph. Celebrate it, live it, plunge into its visions, words, tunes, and pictures. The composite gives a simple and profound result in our souls, not a playful savoring of the past, a little comfort here, a small consolation there, and so much childlike reminiscing. It is the sound of the organ of eternity that involves us and carries us forward, and faith becomes a dynamic power, not soothing, but propelling us irresistibly in mighty, supernatural rhythms. Certainly our crib and customs have their place, and nobody will take them away; but their place is the foreground, the emotional, historical, meditative side of our religious being. Still, while the world moves on in powerful strides and groans for redemption, let us not forget that it was not the Babe Who redeemed it, but the Babe grown Man, crucified, resurrected, and sitting at the right hand of the Father, whence He will come to *judge* the living and the dead.

Thus, after the more gentle portals of Christmas are passed, and Nativity-Advent has raised us a step nearer to the Son of Man in His mysteries, we shall be able to understand the most majestic of all His feasts: Theophany, when His Godhead shines through His humanity and the Church sings: "Rise, be light, Jerusalem, for thy Light is come and the Glory of the Lord is risen upon thee. . . ." "Upon a high throne I saw a *Man* sitting, whom the multitude of spirits adore, singing together: Behold Him, the name of whose *empire* is to *eternity*."

THE TREASURES OF CHRISTMAS

The Roman celebration of the Nativity found in our missals is based on the Nativity celebration in Bethlehem and Jerusalem. That is the first thing to keep in mind if we are to make the most of the rich repast of liturgy offered us in our Christmas worship. We should also remember that we have only half a Christmas if we do not also keep in mind the Epiphany with its great mystery. Like Good Friday and the Easter Vigil, Christmas and Epiphany belong together and explain each other.

Both Christmas and Epiphany have three Masses. The three Masses of Epiphany are now spread over three different days (January 6th, 13th, and the Sunday following), but on the Feast of the Nativity the three Masses are all on the same day. Most of us, however, are not aware of an important feature—that these three Masses are to be celebrated in three different places. The Mass at midnight is to be offered at the crib in St. Mary Major, the Mass at dawn at the church of St. Anastasia at the Palatine Hill, and the last and most solemn Mass at the main altar of St. Mary Major (originally, however, at St. Peter's).

Why the choice of these three churches? According to the best hypothesis, Rome tried to imitate the usage of Jerusalem at a period shortly after the emancipation of the Church by the edicts of Constantine. Many pilgrims came back from the Holy Land with reports on the celebration of the sacred events in the life of Our Lord in the very places where they had taken place.

In Jerusalem that meant a Midnight Mass at the place of the crib in Bethlehem, where the imperial family had erected a great basilica. In Rome its substitute was the large shrine of the Blessed Mother that contained the relics of the crib, according to tradition. From Bethlehem the pilgrims walked to the Sanctuary of the Resurrection, called in Greek the *Anastasis*. There the Mass was to be sung at dawn, the time of the "resurrection" of the sun, the most powerful symbol of the victorious Christ. The Roman *Anastasis* was a replica built on an equivocation: the Church of St. Anastasia, the virgin martyr, a sanctuary near the imperial palace and very convenient for the courtiers and the Greek colony living at the imperial court. The several texts of this Mass that refer to light and speak of radiance were chosen purposely for this Mass at sunrise.

The third Mass in Jerusalem was held at the cathedral. It was the principal and most solemn celebration and therefore the most profoundly theological. In Rome the most popular church, embodying the fondest memories of local pride, was the one erected so recently as a *martyrium*—a witness memorial—over the grave of Peter. The Mass texts gave splendor to the full meaning of the Incarnation by reaching beyond its historical details. In later ages another consideration moved this third Mass to where it is today: the main sanctuary of St. Mary Major, the shrine of the *Theotokos*, the Mother of God, whose human assent was the divinely fashioned instrument of the Incarnation so fully hymned in the first chapter of Hebrews and in the first chapter of John's Gospel, both of which are read on this day.

Added to this is Psalm 97, so pregnant with majesty and eternity, echoing through the Introit, the Gradual responsory, and the Communion procession, and the result is one of the most powerful compositions of the normally powerful and virile liturgy of the city of

Rome, which is also our own. It is obvious, then, that we miss the point of this ancient trilogy of Masses, if we perform them like "three of the same," one after the other. They come to life for us, plastically and in their symbolical meaning, only at the times appointed for them, at midnight, at dawn, and in the morning.

No doubt the Midnight Mass, with its intimate beauty, has become closest to the heart of the people. Its Gospel is most consoling, and contains the message that all Christians accept as the inspiration of the whole festal season. Generations that look for idylls, and not for great visions, have too often overlooked, however, the full liturgical significance of the Midnight Mass. The Psalms chosen for it hardly support the sentimentality with which the Midnight Mass is often surrounded. Rather, the chords that rise from these Psalms boom and resound with strength and give a background of eternity, of kingdom, of strife and of victory to the sweet texts of the readings.

When the clergy enter the church the music is set to the words of the martial Psalm 2. Not only is it a thought of eternity, "The Lord said to me: thou art my Son, I have begotten Thee today," that raises the story of the Gospel into its proper setting, but this antiphon echoes and reechoes thoughts of strife and war: "Why do the heathen rage and the nations devise vain plots?" Here we have the complete, not the fragmentary, aspect of the Nativity. It is not meant to serve as an escape into a golden past. When the music of the Latin words is stripped off, the Epistle, in its plain English, says: deny worldly desire and live soberly, justly and godly; look for the coming of the great God and Savior; He gave Himself to cleanse us.

This is followed by an excerpt from Psalm 109 in the Gradual which, after an attentive hearing of the Epistle and before the "presence" of Christ in the words of His Gospel, serves to focus our thoughts; even in translation it is not idyllic, but filled with a reality that surpasses all nature: "With Thee is royal power on the day of Thy power: in the splendor of Holies have I begotten Thee from my loins before the morning star: The Lord said to my Lord: sit at my right hand until I make thy enemies the footstool of Thy feet."

Then, as a preparation for the Gospel, its theological "level" is set by the threefold Alleluia that contains again the words: "The Lord said to me: Thou art my Son, I have begotten Thee today."

These psalms have the impact of their Christian meaning, not that of the Hebrew original. They are here not so much the cries of souls groping for God, but, like marble columns taken from ancient buildings and reshaped to serve their new purpose of building the spiritual mansion of the divine in humanity, they are triumphant statements of the unfathomable mystery that emerged with the Nativity into the vision of man.

They have become so much a part of the liturgy that, where they occur in it, it would be vain to replace them with versions "truer to the original." They were chosen for the obvious and typical meaning when they were reset in the crown of worship. The psalms and canticles, the prophecies and Old Testament quotations used in the Mass are not there for their authenticity and accuracy to prove a dogma, but to express the faith assumed by all and presumed to have inspired the choice of the little stones out of which the mosaic of words is composed. And this mosaic of texts clamors for its music, its liturgical execution, its celebrating congregations, its interpretation in chant and gesture, and for the word of the preacher who is to interpret it. Only in its totality does it convey the full meaning of this great feast, of which the crib is only a partial, although a central glimpse of the whole.

With this wealth at our disposal, every year for more than a thousand years, why is it that we are dogged today by a secularized Christmas of office parties and Santa Clauses, with ad men's and salesmen's Christmases outside our churches? Why the little inanities with carols inside? Where is the impact of those powerful prophecies, the turning of the minds, the *metanoeite* of St. John, our spiritual guide through Advent? In the name of this feast and in the power of its grace, who cannot but turn his face toward the future instead of lingering in escapist dreams about his childhood memories? Yet why is it all lost, not only on the people, but all too often upon their leaders, lay and clerical, who seem almost blind to the images our liturgy not only conjures up before our minds, but even fulfills with sacramental reality. These texts should heat the metal of our souls for the grace to forge it into a new image, but it all goes by—charitably dismissed as at best an esthete's revery. But why?

One of the answers is so simple that few think of it: because it is all in Latin. Having a translation in one's hands to watch it is not the same as singing or as listening without the need of an interpreter, as it were; and it is not the same as immediacy in celebration. How can one be all ear and eye, when he has to flip pages and keep track of texts? Besides the "people of the book," in this case, will always be the few, maybe the elect.

Whether the vernacular translations have the sonorous tunefulness of the Latin or will always lack this quality is irrelevant as long as the Latin is, in effect, a mute beauty that is mutely admired—mere sound to entrance the listener without speaking to him. The angels above Bethlehem's field did not sing, in celestial idiom, an unknown text; the shepherds heard in their language the "Glory to God in the highest and peace on earth to men of good will."

Esthetically, the blend of Gregorian chant with the words *"In splendoribus Sanctorum ante luciferum genui te,"* sung while the faithful receive in Holy Communion the Incarnate Son Whom this Psalm so plastically glorifies, is superb—for him to whom it is more than mere sound. But an adequate English version: "In the splendor of the Holies before the morning star I have begotten Thee," together with its Psalm, pierces mere hearing and stamps the soul with a live image of the coming Savior. We need all the beauty that is at man's command to feast this mystery, but we are in equal need of the truth, and truth is not conveyed by rationally mute sound.

The most powerful medicine against shallow sentimentalism, which breeds secularism, is the Word coming on wings of grace. "In these times God has spoken to us with a Son to speak for Him; . . . Through Him. . . . He created the world of time; a Son who is the radiance of His Father's splendor and the full expression of His being. . . . Lord, Thou hast laid the foundations of the earth at its beginning and the heavens are the work of Thy hands. They will perish, but Thou wilt remain; they will all be like a cloak that grows threadbare and Thou wilt lay them aside like a garment and exchange them for new; but Thou art He who never changes; Thy years will not come to an end" (from the Epistle of the Third Mass). This thunder is echoed by John in the Gospel. In English, they will be drunk deep, like a draft of clear water. They will prepare the soul better than man-made aspirations to receive the Bread of Life.

PAROUSIA

Parousia is a strange term of Greek origin unknown to the general Catholic public, yet it is one of the "fullest" terms of our Christian language. Simply explained, it means the "Presence" of Christ on the Last Day, His second coming. But it means this in all its connotations and implications, and it is in this wide range of signification that I have called it "full."

In order to understand it well, we have to recall a great many things that have slipped out of the minds of the average modern Catholic and that will have to be retrieved in painful labor, especially from the liturgical documents of the Church, from the Acts of Martyrs, from early Christian writers and, above all, from the New Testament. This scientific work was done by the well-known scholar Dom Odo Casel, the Benedictine monk of the abbey of Maria Laach. To him we owe the careful investigation that enables us now to speak of parousia in a simple, popular way. This conception, especially in its liturgical realization, is very fruitful for all those who want to reach a profound understanding of the liturgy of the Church, and of her sacramental life. It is the key to a great many of its present problems. Much of it is now for the multitude either a venerable relic or a quaint garment of things that are unrelated to our modern spiritual lives.

In the first place, we have to make one indispensable change in our common attitude toward Christ's second coming. We have inherited from the high Middle Ages an attitude that is almost exclusively one of fear. Jacopone da Todi's *"Dies irae, dies illa"* is as eloquent a witness of this feeling as Michelangelo's "Last Judgment" in the Sistine Chapel. It is a feeling of terror and fright. The terrible day of wrath and revenge. *"Quid sum miser tunc dicturus?"* "What shall I wretched one then say?" All the consolation of redemption seems to have gone from the grand fresco in the papal chapel. Even Mary is stricken with terror and cowers in fear. Peter clutches his keys and holds them up, terror in his eyes. Before a Pope of the post-Renaissance had a second-rate artist paint clothes on Christ and the saints the stark nudity made this great painting a still more horrifying sight.

No wonder we would rather not hear too much of the parousia except in a mission or retreat, when these visions are used to instill in us a wholesome terror and a consequent aim to work out our salvation in fear and trembling. Great ascetics in every century have recommended the day of reckoning to our frequent consideration, for our love of God and of good is so weak that we need the whip of possible damnation to keep us on the narrow path or bring us back to it. Christ's own parables are not squeamish in their language of warning.

Yet it was He who said: "Lift up your heads, because your redemption is near." From the Apostles on, especially through Peter's and Paul's Epistles and John's Apocalypse, the prevailing spirit is one of longing for the great day of Christ's return: "Maranatha, come, Lord Jesus." In every vigil celebration, especially the "Great Night" of Easter Saturday and of the Ember Saturdays, Christians, Catholics, dedicated themselves to the celebration of this spirit of longing expectation for Christ's second coming, His parousia. These night-long vigils, now anticipated on Easter Saturday mornings, had their climax in what was then called simply the "Great Mysteries," now briefly, the Mass. In it Christ became present, first spiritually in the Gospel, and after that, sacramentally under the symbols of bread and wine to nourish His faithful for another period of expectation. Every one of these vigils, of these watches in the night till the sun rose over the Sacred Species on the altars of Christendom, these fasts, these celebrations of singing and reading were little "parousias."

The element of fear was, of course, there too, since only perfect love is able to cast it out (St. John). But above this there were hope and longing and joy. Our individualism makes us think about nothing but our own soul and its salvation. Without succumbing to collectivism and its sinister consequences, our fathers had a more communal attitude and a fuller consciousness of being members of a whole, the *Ekklesia Christou;* of being the ones who had been called from out of the mass of mankind to be living members of the Anointed One, the Christ. The fate of this Christ, of His Body, was what supremely filled their minds and, seeing themselves as the People of God, the homebound ship of Christ, what was more natural for them than to see their King return to His people and the ship anchored in its eternal harbor?

How did it happen that succeeding generations gradually slipped into a sectional, partial view of this great mystery? How did we lose our otherworldliness from our philosophy of life, we might ask?

There are several reasons that deserve mention. The history of the sociological and psychological development of piety has not yet been written from the viewpoint of correct scientific research and in the spirit of faith. There are only scattered observations in books of history and sociology, written mostly, however, by non-Catholics. Yet, while the dogmatic and liturgical structure has been preserved intact by the assistance of the Holy Spirit, there are many facts that point to the emphasis having shifted from a total, communal, Christocentric attitude to the present popular one of sectional, individualistic, and anthropocentric sentiment.

What then were the reasons for this loss of the fullness of the parousia? There is, first, the lapse from the Church of the martyrs to the powerful institution following A.D. 313, with its mass conversions and its lowering of standards which then had to be rescued and preserved in the monastic orders and the liturgical books. Once opportunists and people "born with a church" forming part of their civic life became a majority, enthusiasm, the mother soil of the parousia spirit, and high moral standards, its atmosphere, were lowered. The saltiness of the Faith, which Christ had given as a condition for its survival, had to be preserved in reservations: the celibate clergy, the monastic orders, and the poor. The art of making of earth as comfortable a place as possible and still retaining a minimum of religion developed more and more for the average man of means in all walks of ecclesiastical life.

Those masses could not be moved by enthusiasm and love, so they had to be moved by fear, and fear was what they got from their worried shepherds. No wonder that the parousia was scarcely seen in its full outline. We really know only the things that impress us and are part of our lives. A vision that does not materialize in our pattern of life fades into theory, to which we may pay eager lip service, but which will not be an "existential truth," a truth integrated into our person.

Another reason is the growing ignorance of the masses in the Dark Ages and their crude way of thinking. Anything as complex as the full conception of the parousia would have to be ignored, and the nearby whip of fear was more important in the laborious and gradual education of Franks and Celts and Saxons, Burgundians and Slavs and Magyars.

Thirdly, there seems to be a certain relish in gloom among Nordic nations, whether Celtic or Germanic or Slavic. None of their native religions is characterized by serene and light traits, and they were products of their national characters. No wonder that this component of their character should linger on until our own day. It was the North that forced black vestments on the Church for funerals, not Rome, where the Pope alone still wears purple at the Requiem. These little, apparently unimportant things show the general drift of thought. The fierce, bloody times from the collapse of the Empire to the disasters of the late Middle Ages may also have something to do with it. Yet, no one can say that it was all sweetness and glory before, certainly not during the first three hundred years. The real explanation is probably that the spiritual conquest of disastrous happenings requires greater maturity and Christian integration than the young convert nations possessed, while antiquity had a natural heritage of wisdom, on which grace built its lofty edifice.

The great hindrance in the way of grasping this idea of triumph and joy, of victory in death, of resurrection, was of a different kind after the Renaissance: skepticism, growing material wealth, secularism, "this-worldly" utopias, bourgeois optimism and trust in the endless progress of civilization. All these hindered the already weakened seed of a complete and total faith from maturing. The very idea of faith as the dynamo, not the soothing drug of life; the burning spirit of propulsion, instead of the consoling cushion for the deathbed; this very idea was faint. No wonder nobody saw any stirring message in the parousia! As a matter of fact, apart from the Church's adamant teaching of it and the longing of a few saints and holy people, who wanted Christ to come back and make an end of it all? What was the Kingdom of Heaven to men who were either plainly secularized or, if spiritual, interested only in individual souls, and I say "souls" instead of men, women, and children?

And yet we have an enormous and living monument of this spirit of the parousia in our midst, of the coming of the Lord. It is the feast of the Epiphany and the things built around it. If we learn to celebrate, to "realize" it, its fullness will again transform our souls and counteract the human obstacles that have heretofore stood in its way.

The Feast of the Epiphany, in our modern popular estimation, takes only second place after Christmas. As a matter of fact it has been degraded to the Feast of the "Three Wise Men," as if it were nothing but that. What is it in fact?

A feast is best understood by the mysteries it contains, as they are found in its liturgical texts. Now this very feast has one antiphon that summarizes its content. It is the antiphon of the *Benedictus,* the hymn of Zachary that the priestly choirs sing at sunrise in the hour of Lauds before Mass is celebrated. *"Hodie Coelesti Sponso . . ."* "Today the Church is being united to the Heavenly Bridegroom, as in Jordan Christ washes off her sins, the Magi come running with gifts to the royal wedding, and the guests feast on wine made out of water." We find this same thought in a rhymed version in the hymn sung at sundown during the Vesper hour. Thus, we discover three motifs in this feast: the visit of the Magi, Christ's baptism by St. John in the Jordan, and the wedding feast of Cana. As a matter of fact these three Gospels are actually read during the celebration of the feast, on January 6th and 13th. It is probable that originally they were read more closely together. There is normally one Sunday between January 6th and 13th. The Gospel for this Sunday (now suppressed by the Feast of the Holy Family) shows us the boy Jesus in the temple, enthroned (Introit) among the wise elders of His nation, questioning and teaching them.

The connecting thought or ideal unity of all four of these Gospels is the manifestation of the Godhead in Christ to the Magi, to the elders, to His forerunner, and finally to His apostles in His first miracle (Cana). This feast apparently came from Alexandria in Egypt, where it was first known to be celebrated. That accounts for its richness, its profundity, and its subtlety of composition. To us it seems a far cry from "manifestation" to "heavenly wedding," and yet those of us who read our Old Testament understand what it means when it says: "Adam *knew* Eve," "Abraham *knew* Sara," or "David did not *know* the Sulamites." Does not even the New Testament say of Joseph: "and he did not know her (Mary) till she had brought forth her firstborn son" (Matt. 1:25)? In the profundity of Greek and Oriental minds the progresses of cognition and generation, though in different spheres, were alike. Creative joy connotes both. So, when God "manifests" Himself to His chosen among men and to the world alike, in tremendous miracles; when He and man *know* each other in Christ, the Infant, the Boy, the Man, the Power, then this is indeed a wedding.

The key to this mystical composition of hymns, introits, graduals, and psalms—this full reality, the symbolic guide—is the seasons before and after, especially those two thundering Sundays (the last after Pentecost; the first of Advent) which have as their Gospels the announcement of the parousia. They are prophecy, spoken by Christ. January 6th and its companions in this constellation are the "pre-reality," the pledge that the parousia is true, is real, because God has already manifested Himself, and His Godhead shone through one human Life in four symbolic visions. Read the texts, the antiphons, the epistles, the hymns from the Eighteenth Sunday after Pentecost on, and see the gradual swelling of a wave of hope and joy and expectation. It is a mighty, distinct chorus in Advent. The great prelude is given on Christmas, and we rest for a while in the Incarnation. But this is not yet the terminus. Like a theme of Beethoven, the mighty motif asserts itself with renewed force until it breaks out in full splendor on the day of *Theophania*. Its joy, its richness, its triumph show us what our true calling is. Christ the Victor. "Arise, be light, O Jerusalem: for thy light is come and the glory of the Lord is risen upon thee. For, behold darkness shall cover the earth and a mist the people: but the Lord shall arise upon thee and his glory shall be seen upon thee." Light, the star, wine, the bride and bridegroom, water, the *cathedra* in the temple, the three gifts, all these express joy and richness. It is the richness of Christ's coming. No mere statement in so many words can convey all the aspects of the kaleidoscopic deployment of what we contemplate with longing and love: Parousia, Maranatha, come, Lord Jesus.

5

Liturgy and the Arts

FASHIONS IN CHURCH ARCHITECTURE*

Architectural styles come and go, and the Church has canonized none of them. Gothic and baroque have seemed to acquire a semi-official approval but this is only apparently so. Inevitably there comes a day when a daring prince of the Church wants a "modern" church building. It happened in the Middle Ages when Romanesque and Gothic minsters were torn down to make room for new Gothic and Renaissance temples—"modern" churches. It is happening again today all over the world. As long as there is a spark of vitality in any civilization, it will look for novel expressions of its faith. We need be afraid only if all the daring and novelty go into secular efforts, if all the money, all the artistic effort, all the planning go into new gigantic structures of this world, and the houses of God become anemic, repetitious, ivory towers of bygone times, escapes from our own time into a glorified past. Then, indeed, there may be some reason for fear!

But the style of a church in itself is not "liturgical." As long as a church complies with canon law and rubrics, even if it were a nightmare of bad taste and poor architecture, it is "liturgical." Of course, there is such a thing as being more or less liturgical. If you cannot see the altar or follow the Mass well, if you cannot hear the preacher, or if your baptistry is an off-corner job not conducive to a real appreciation of the sacrament, then your church is less liturgical—be it a

* See my pamphlet, "Speaking of Liturgical Architecture," Notre Dame Liturgy Program Publication, Notre Dame, Indiana, 1952.

Byzantine basilica full of marble and mosaics, or a Gothic poem of masonry and stained glass of the deepest blue and most glowing red.

The liturgical church is simply a church that puts first things first. This means in our times an almost revolutionary change, not in style only, but in the organization of its parts. With our growing understanding of sacramental theology and its meaning for the life of the individual and the community, we need churches that in structure and ornament are a true reflection of sacramental values. A church building that is cluttered up with non-essentials or in which sacramental observances and devotional practices obtrude upon each other lacks the clarity of conception that is needed to show forth its true meaning, and is insofar unliturgical.

The place where we celebrate the mystery of the Mass, which is of the sacramental order, is obviously not the most suitable place for private devotions, at least not without harming the clear distinction between the two. To relegate the baptistry to a corner or an unimportant side chapel does not show forth the meaning of Baptism and its relation, or rather the character of its relation, to the Holy Eucharist.

The main altar should be the focal point of the church, and it should be an altar that shows forth its character as the place of sacrifice and as a banquet table. Its real ornament is what is done on it: the Mysteries. The rubrical demands are an example of typically Roman moderation: a crucifix and six candles. The earlier we get away from reredos and hangings behind and around the altar— the antependium of course excepted—the better we shall bring to prominence the really important thing, the altar.

Since we stress the educational value of our architecture, let us have only one altar in sight of the entire congregation, and let it be strongly emphasized by the architectural lines. The images should likewise direct attention to the altar. Let us again have Christ's image dominating, with Our Lady in due proportion, and the saints also in their proper scale. The patron saint should, for instance, be near the main altar, and the order in the choice of saints ought to be taken from the liturgy celebrated in this very church. A Sacred Heart statue on the same level and scale with any saint is certainly a rather unthinking manifestation of dogmatic confusion and liturgical naïveté.

The Stations of the Cross, shrines, and popular images are also on a different level. They do not belong to the Mysteries of the Church in the *cultual* sense. The stations are means of meditation and historical reminiscence, interwoven with tradition and legend. Our attitude when we pray them is altogether different from our attitude when we celebrate the Mysteries of Christ, the *opus operatum*. Therefore they should be in a special chapel that provides the kind of atmosphere our people want for such occasions. This chapel should contain, too, shrines of our sodalities and confraternities, of novenas and special devotions. If we can get permission to do so, we could also have the Blessed Sacrament reserved in this or in another chapel for private adoration (as is done in St. Peter's and in most of the churches of Rome and Italy). Since our afternoon devotions seem to attract fewer and fewer people, such a smaller chapel could provide the intimacy which those require who frequent them. A good architect can easily prevent such a chapel from becoming a sort of liturgical "horror chamber" crowded with all sorts of things purged from the "Eucharistic main church." Many church buildings have in use a "lower church" open all day for private devotion. My only objection to this practice is the customary closing in some areas of the upper church except on Sundays—so that the faithful cannot enter and pray where the main altar stands, the center and source of the parish life.

Two things remain to be discussed: the place of the baptistry and that of the confessionals. All these parts of the church structure should not only be clearly distinct within the church, but should be visible as distinct parts in the building's outward architecture.

Since Baptism is the sacrament of initiation, it should be given near the gates of the church. The baptistry should correspond to the sanctuary in its location, its majesty, and its beauty. Its size should be such that solemn administration of the sacrament of Baptism will be easy. Every Baptism starts at the gate, has a procession, ceremonies before the inner sanctum of the baptistry: Where is there a baptistry that takes account of all this and of the dignity of the sacrament? Have our architects built churches that remind us that we all have entered the Church through Baptism, that the very holy water stoops are reminders of Baptism? All these things should find their physical and realistic expression in the architecture. The gate of the church, the baptistry and the "lustral water" that we take on entering the church should be close together spatially, as well as in design, in scale, and in architectural integration. If any interpretation of the rubrics permits it, why not return to the cantharus with constantly flowing fresh water, "living water" so to speak? Especially since the average holy-water stoop is hardly representative of cleansing water. The Church can certainly bless running water as well as stagnant water—She blesses rivers and She also allows us to add water repeatedly to already blessed holy and baptismal water.

The confessionals should be located away from the main body, that is, the central and side aisles or the transept of the church. Penance is a renewal of Baptism. The chapel containing confessionals ought therefore to be near the baptistry, perhaps even in it. This is educationally important. Too many faithful still link the Holy Eucharist with confession as a permanent and inseparable unit—a leftover of crypto-Jansenism, or the mentality which prevailed before Pius X's Communion decrees. There are a dozen practical reasons that would make it preferable to have the confessionals in a unit distinct from the "Eucharistic church"—for example, heating, disturbance of Sunday Mass, lighting. None of them is so important as the liturgical reason of visible logical distinctness. But what about tradition? Did not confession take place at the altar rail? Does not forgiveness of sins flow from the Cross and the Sacrifice of Calvary? Both questions can be answered, I think.

The second is easier. We are dealing here with liturgy, not with dogma as dogma. Otherwise, since Baptism flows from the Cross as well, we would have to baptize in the sanctuary. Liturgy is our way of life, not a theoretical structure. The Mysteries of cult require therefore a different "order" from the dogmatic and systematic disposition of theoretical theology. In our way of life, Baptism is the gate, Penance is reentrance, is lustration, cleansing, the *via purgativa,* while Communion is the climax, the *via unitiva.* Therefore these things in their logical order of life should be visibly separated, so that even those whom St. Augustine calls the *"rudes"* can see and grasp the organic coherence, perspective, and relation of things.

That confession once was made at the altar rail is a historical fact—although I do not know how long this custom prevailed and how universal it was. But it is equally certain that this practice obtained when confession was a rarer thing than it is nowadays, and its technique was less developed than it is with us. Probably for reasons of privacy and to protect the individual, it was moved away from such a conspicuous place. Its present location seems to be just a matter of practical convenience—where else could one put two, four, or six bulky wooden structures but in the side aisles, or transept, or the rear of the church? That does not mean that they have to remain there forever. If we now see better the relations of one sacrament to another, and of the sacraments to life, if our present practice of frequent, devotional confession advises an improvement, and if it would serve to counteract a mistaken idea in the minds of many devout faithful—why not make a change? True tradition is a growing, living stream of integration and discernment, not petrifaction and glacial arrest! The Church moves and lives.

We shall have liturgical churches, not so much by improvement of taste alone, but by functional construction and trueness to new materials! It is not even sufficient to apply the "four causes" of Aristotle to the planning and building—unless our final cause includes the firm purpose of making the building a clear, eloquent witness of the new spirit that is moving to reestablish the sacramental cosmos of the Church.

ART, ARCHITECTURE, AND THE CHRISTIAN

In 1938, in *Architectural Forum*, I published an article on modern Church architecture that carried an illustration of Rudolf Schwartz's arresting little church at Leversbach in the Rhineland, built a few years earlier. It is one of those spare and frugal pieces of architecture which at that time our generation found so difficult to accept but which from the architects' point of view is most inspiring. How slowly such architecture is accepted became evident when the same church was pictured in *Worship* in February, 1958 to illustrate the latest development in church architecture. A church more than a quarter of a century old was used as an example of the new, progressive, and advanced design in which we are trying to interest the Catholic of our day! Certainly there is something wrong somewhere, either with the new buildings or the architects or the public they serve. This is particularly puzzling at a time when modern buildings on Park Avenue, in San Francisco's Bay area, and in other cities are readily accepted. Religion, in the popular mind, is thought to have no fashions, no changes; it should not have to undergo rethinking: that has all been settled for most of us by what is loosely called "tradition." But here we are on the threshold of our first discovery:

There have always been changing fashions in church building; the only constant tradition is that of change.

We know very little about ecclesiastical architecture until the Church became free in A.D. 313 under Constantine. But if we look at the architectural history of Western and Northern Europe, we find roughly these periods in church building: four hundred years of basilica style; two hundred years (more or less) of Romanesque; four hundred years, overlapping at both ends, of Gothic style; about two hundred years of Renaissance style which gradually evolved into baroque and rococo, and at last into what is called "classicism." Just as it is hard to say when one season of the year ends and another begins, so it is difficult to give the exact end of one architectural style and the beginning of another. Are the Norman churches budding Gothic or dying Romanesque? Is the cathedral of Florence late Gothic or early Renaissance? How should we characterize the Northwest German cathedrals with their pointed Gothic arches and their Romanesque-looking thick walls and small windows? Style is in constant motion, period following period, and what was progressive yesterday is old-fashioned and worn out tomorrow. Even technical discoveries, like the pointed arch and its resultant effect on walls and vaulted ceilings, have had their influence on changing styles: what was possible in ages past cannot simply be thrown out now.

But technological advance in itself did not create new styles. New techniques alone might have remained unnoticed by church builders had not a new spirituality come forth simultaneously with their discovery. There is more than coincidence in the fact that just when Romanesque solidity had run its course and it had become technically possible to construct towering lacelike buildings with much stained glass breaking up solid walls, a freshening wave of sublime mysticism and theological speculation swept through the Western world. The new religious impulse expressed itself naturally in architecture, sculpture, and painting. It is evident to us now that the cathedrals of France and the *Summae* of St. Thomas Aquinas are related, but should we assume that such a subtle relationship might occur only once, or would we not be wiser to look for it again as a possibility in the twentieth century?

A glance at the past has helped to bring our vision of the present into focus. We realize that there is an everlasting change in religious art: this truth is the first fruit of our present discussion.

The second result of our reflection is that this ever-changing movement of the arts has spiritual as well as technical and sociological causes. May we not discern a certain relationship between the post-medieval interest in man and loss of emphasis on God and the naturalism of the Renaissance masters and their glorification of physical beauty of supposedly Greek inspiration? The humanism of the Renaissance was largely a Christian humanism, but it was not the inward- and upward-looking spirit that inspired Chartres, Nuremberg, or Assisi.

That there should be two tendencies, one preserving what exists and the other striding along new paths in all that concerns the life of the Church, is not only a reflection of nature's way, but was predicted by our Lord Himself, when He used two parables to illustrate the growth of the Church: the parable of the mustard seed indicating slow and regular growth; the parable of the leaven, illustrating the internal upheaval, the turmoil, and the explosiveness of change.

There are different principles at play in different styles, yet certain old principles recurring in new works are often hard to recognize. For instance, one of the most striking features of such masterpieces as Chartres or Freiburg is the soaring quality, the triumph of spirit over matter, the almost absolute disembodying of the stone that is accomplished without leaving the structure less human or alive. In seeing a Gothic cathedral one is reminded of a slender, tall, and yet sturdy tree, tongueless, of course, yet singing its "sursum corda" by sheer dynamic form.

There is an echo of this vibrant spirituality in the best of modern churches: thick walls are no longer needed for sturdy support; walls have become thin veils to cover the holy and to exclude the grime and dust of the world outside. An authentic contemporary church, to distinguish it from poorly contrived pseudo-modern pretenses, has something of this otherworldliness: it is a pilgrim's church of almost tent-like fragility. There is little fat on the bones of the Gothic church; all is muscle and sinew showing the skeleton in its outline. This again is the case with our present churches of steel, concrete, wood, and glass; still, there are differences caused by the new ease of construction and the new outlook of the spirit itself. No longer does the outline of the church soar vertically to heaven; the Church in our day is burdened with the task of remolding the world in the image of Christ by entering into its life. Instead of withdrawing from the life of the world, she tries to reintegrate the spirit of man;

instead of employing splendor to symbolize an empire parallel to the world's, she comes in chaste and pure humility, tenting among the disinherited people of our day.

A strange contrast the Church provides to the pride of ill-clad and ill-housed Russian workers strutting through the bronze and marble splendor of the Moscow subway stations: the simple modern church is here to lead men home to God, while the subway, for all its magnificence, only carries them back to drab shacks and apartments or to grimy factories. Faith in nothing but a coming earthly paradise (long in coming, to say the least) is far less firmly based than is our faith in a merciful Judge and Redeemer.

Our modern churches also reflect an element of the Romanesque, again provided they are truly modern and not superficial adaptations of worn-out patterns. It is present in the joy of clean, original shapes: cubes, cones, sloping surfaces, the sharply delineated meeting of straight walls, and is manifested in the interplay of light and shadow, of pure white and primary colors. The joy of the rather primitive yet original builder is apparent here as it was toward the beginning of the eleventh century, when creative energies were being released by a new society emerging from feudalism. Certainly there are enormous differences between such wonders as Cluny, Maria Laach, and St. Zeno in Verona and the first halting steps of modern church building: Corpus Christi in Aachen, St. Anthony's in Basel, and St. Charles in Lucerne; but a sensitive eye can see in them the exhilaration of a new beginning. All bear in common the signature of frugality: no fat and ostentation, only spare and simple ornament. Pure shapes and forms, the prime elements of construction, are beautiful in themselves.

Like the basilica, our modern churches are centered on the two mysteries of rebirth and growth, Baptism and the Eucharist. In Gothic cathedrals liturgy is sunk at the bottom of a sacred sea of soaring forms, a small plant surrounded by large trees. We are swept upward by the striking features of this style: it is the architecture of the lone mystic communing with God without community or sacrament. In the Romanesque minsters, on the other hand, the liturgy of the Church has become an affair of the clergy to be performed on a high stage in grandeur and majesty; participation is entirely through the eye's enraptured gaze. But for a true sense of participation we must return to the style of the first basilicas which had the Mass in the people's language—Greek or Latin—with a continuous interchange between altar and nave in responses, common singing, processions at the Introit, the Gospel, the Offertory, and the Communion. Authentic modern churches share these features with the oldest known examples of church architecture.

Whether a church is truly modern or only overlaid with modern trappings that catch the eyes is infallibly tested by the floor plan. The cross shape of an ordinary parish church can only be seen from a helicopter and can hardly be appreciated by the congregation inside. As a form it creates waste space and injects symbolism just where one is least able to grasp it. It is a completely nonfunctional floor plan that splits the congregation into three parts; it is a striking example of symbolistic piety misapplied.

A useful floor plan is one that keeps the focal principals—the altar and the baptismal font—in dominant positions, each with its appropriate space. The congregation should be outside the sanctuary, which is reserved to the sacred ministers, and yet should be close to the altar and have a full view. It would not be right to place the altar in the center of the church because the priest could never face the whole congregation either in prayer or sermon; like a bull ring or a boxing arena, such an arrangement would tend to create merely spectators, not participants. (In this sense, the circular floor plan with the altar in the middle is quite opposed to the spirit of the liturgy.)

A series of questions, along with a few remarks, may enable the reader to decide whether or not the church his parish is considering achieves the modern ideal in architecture.

Is it in its inspiration representative of the apostolic and consecrating spirit, which is the Church's spirit at all times?

Is it truly organized: are its parts organically distinct? Does it show by its structure inside and out that it is meant for the meeting of the congregational, hierarchically organized Body of Christ and the celebration of His Mysteries? Is the main body of the church truly "an upper room" free of distracting accessories? Are baptistry and confessionals coordinated? Have smaller, more intimate chapels been provided for individual devotions? In other words, is the separation of the different functions visible, and easy to recognize?

Apart from its liturgical functions, how will the new church serve as a monument to faith, as a part of the city and of the landscape: how does it fit into the surrounding architecture; is the building appropriate to its particular site, and does it realistically reflect the economic and social conditions of the parishioners? Have local building materials been put to skillful use?

Does something about the building say its purpose is a supernatural one? Is it built in a style that is not outlandish, foreign, or pseudo-traditional, but with the rich means provided by modern technical advance? Is the shock of its newness a salutary one, jarring the complacent out of their rut?

Is the church "uncluttered"? Does it emphasize space, leaving room for the eye to see the essential? The church's gift to the eye is the liturgy in its stately performance; statues, paintings, and murals can only provide the background in a structure composed around the two basic mysteries of initiation and growth: Baptism and the Eucharist. A naked, whitewashed wall may be a better background for the celebration of Mass than marble, stained glass, bronze, and works of intricate design.

Does the church show a truly Christian spirit of poverty? (A dignified poverty, not shoddiness or destitution.) Or is ostentation to be paid for by grinding the faces of the poor through mortgage-paying generations of both priests and parishioners? Will the visible "splendor" of the new church reduce the primary activity of the parish for generations to the chores of raising money for principal and interest? Or is this church (as it well might be) a temporary shelter, a tent of the migratory Christ and His flock, and one which shows that we have no abiding city here below? Why should suburban churches not be built to serve for the time the suburb lasts?

Frugality is a relative term: what is frugal in America may be wealth in India, but in all places it avoids waste and ostentation like fire. God is not served by lavish display: frugality is a challenge to good artists and builders and achieves great things without waste. It is a virtue that also shows compassion for our generation of insecure, struggling migratory wage earners who build, live near, and come to worship in these churches. The modern spirit of frugality forces the planners to deal in essentials; it naturally cuts away all clutter and vulgar display.

The Catholic Church is primarily a missionary Church whose prime obligation is to spread the Word through preaching and sacrament. A certain Gospel-like austerity is therefore most Catholic. The elaborate styles of the Counter Reformation express the wishful thinking of beleaguered and diminished militants. But in the present day, the Church is far less likely to regard Herself as a counterpart to courts and kings and glittering wealth. In its new area of life the Church becomes progressively less extensive and more intensive. The King is hidden and his manifestation is that of Bethlehem, Galilee, and Golgotha.

The spare, slender, light, and open rather than the ponderous, ornate, and cavelike darkness of the past are now the outward symptoms of a radical change. Unfortunately, most new churches still try to display the rich, exuberant theatricality of the baroque period, often with shapes borrowed from historical styles: basilical, Romanesque, or Gothic elements are mingled in a baroque fashion to provide a lavish staging for an inactive, immobilized "audience"; the Mass becomes a tableau to be regarded and not a drama in which the congregation may participate.

What about size? If we have a parish in mind, cathedral-size churches are an evil: they minimize participation, and necessitate a warped liturgy fitted to the needs of crowds, instead of compact liturgical parish families. They make it impossible to establish personal contact between the individual worshiper and Christ on the altar, or between the members of the parish. They make the Church a "religious supermarket and spiritual filling station," in which the priest becomes a purveyor and the faithful, customers. The sacred things become a finished product of priestcraft, not a participation in the Sacred Banquet. Nobody denies that a huge problem is posed when parish "plants" with expensive schools are already in existence and must be maintained; but the small and intimate congregation still remains the ideal. In a mass civilization any further concentration of the crowd is dangerous, especially in the spiritual field. The crowds flowing through our large, double-story churches in and out of hourly Masses have become amorphous, anonymous, impersonal, religiously asphyxiated, starving from unnatural and unnourishing spiritual mass feeding. And this should not be.

The great works of the past may serve as a guide to appreciation of modern decoration. A late example of the earliest mosaics is Monreale Cathedral in Sicily. Here we are put in almost magic awe of the enormous Christ, the saints ranged below Him in hierarchical order. "Distortion" averts the spiritual danger of photographic naturalism. The forms do not bespeak the relaxation of creature comfort, but are taut and rhythmically disposed by a mysterious power that, like grace, starts from nature, but leaves it behind.

The "Christ Returning" found in the tympanon over the main portal of the Romanesque minster of Moissac strikingly illustrates this same principle. The rhythm almost approaches that of Hindu dancing gods, but it is free of sensuous impurity. The distortions are hieratic and cosmic: nature is elevated through an internal rhythm, a movement of grace.

The Belle Verrière of Chartres—and the portal sculpture—also show the elongation and the tenseness of stylized religious art that subtly preserve it from the dangers of naturalistic idolatry. Its colors, however, are of the simplest: strong, pure, and basic.

If we turn to the Renaissance for examples of great religious art, it is not to Michelangelo's Sistine Chapel, with its passionate distortions, its crowds and flesh, where even the Christ and Our Lady were originally depicted as naked Greeks, but to the paintings of

El Greco; here, too, the spirit forces natural lines out of shapes softly pleasing to the eye. All great works of religious art, from the psalms to the cathedrals, have this in common: they point beyond themselves.

The more we really know about God, the more we realize that the human mind cannot comprehend Him: to the Christian believer "God is more, rather than less, mysterious," said Victor White in *God the Unknown*. The finite and plausible art of the bourgeois age is therefore a vastly underrated danger to the basic attitude of mystery and awe which seeks expression in modern Church art as well as in the great works of the past. Our inspiration and that of great builders in the past must flow from a single source, from the spirit of humility, of piety, and of truth.

Those who oppose any change do not want their religion to face the new age: theirs is an escape religion. But escape is hardly even a secondary function of religion. In the first place, we are all called to redeem and consecrate. Rest and consolation are things promised at the last: to seek escape for its own sake is not in the spirit of the Cross but borders dangerously on the Marxist indictment of religion as "a drug of the people." Therefore even in such apparently unimportant matters as style and furnishings of church buildings, if we do not dismiss them altogether—which the traditionalists do not—we must go forward and bear witness to the forward, hopeful, and creative faith that is the Gospel's.

MUSIC IN CHURCH

The old priest who introduced me as a boy into intellectual life by encouraging me to read good magazines was really not my pastor. Our own parish was an hour away, so we went to St. Anthony's. It was in a workingmen's neighborhood and showed an appalling taste in its furnishings, but we liked it because the pastor preached well, we were always sure of a seat, and the walk to church through gardens and open spaces was long and pleasant. Above all, we could sing to our heart's delight: a lusty hymn while the priest hurried through the beginning of the Mass—some favorite and popular hymn like: "Cast down before thy majesty, in dust we Christians cry. . . ." Men, women, and children sang good and loud. When the "doctor," as we called him, had intoned the Latin Gloria we all chimed in (in German, of course, no "outlandish" Latin for us), in "Glory to God in the highest," starting with a melodious shout 'way up on a high note, again after the priest intoned the Creed, when he finished the Preface, and when he said the Agnus Dei. There were more hymns sung to fill the time that was left, some in correspondence with the season, some just favorites.

My father had a beautiful bass voice and had sung these hymns from his boyhood days on. When he had been an altar boy vespers were still sung congregationally and in the people's tongue. My mother was the more musically educated of my parents and she thought the singing was terrible and disliked the hymns. The whole family agreed to disagree on this and we worshiped together, "each in his own words, each in his own way." A Sunday in Hamburg was not a Sunday without our sonorous worship of the Almighty.

The year 1914 brought this to an end for me when I entered the army, and strange to say, my taste changed too, once I realized that these hymns were not only musically inferior, but gave only a faint idea of the great content of the liturgical prototype they replaced. After becoming acquainted with Guardini and Maria Laach, and after spending a year in the seminary at Innsbruck, I became deeply convinced that these hymns at Mass were poor substitutes indeed and that the true fare for the soul and the congregation was the Mass in all its wealth.

Here then is the problem that presented itself during one decade of my life and that is still with us: participation in the Mass as the condition of all other participations that are the ideal of the Christian Church. But what kind and what degree of participation are good? Are there limits set up by education or by tradition, good, bad, and indifferent? Do we have to assume that the people are unable to do more than they do, that they are uneducable, apathetic, and passive?

Just a little more than thirty-two years ago I spent a weekend in Salzburg, Austria. After saying my private Mass in St. Peter's Abbey Church and enjoying a light Austrian breakfast, I walked over to the cathedral, whose metropolitan has the proud title of Primate of Germany, to assist at a Pontifical Mass where one of the great Mozart Masses with solos and orchestra was to be sung. People of all faiths, in their tourist best, crowded the pews for the Kyrie and the magnificent and masterfully executed Gloria, deeply enraptured by the musical treat and, I am sure, in a religious and sacred mood. Many of them went out for a coffee and smoke and then came quietly back to listen to the Credo, the Sanctus, the Agnus Dei, and a motet by the great master. Many music lovers who were also worshipers stayed with the celebrating bishop, who looked rather deserted and neglected in the faraway sanctuary of the largest church north of the Alps. That was music in church.

I have seen tourists in St. Peter's at Rome act in the same way during the Lamentations on Holy Thursday: quieting down for a Palestrina responsorium or a solo by one of the glorious boy sopranos, silent and standing still in awe. Then the moment the singing flattens out into the rapid recitation of the psalms, the murmur of conversation and the movement of groups start again. Music in church.

But then think of Solesmes, Maria Laach, our American abbeys, both Benedictine and Cistercian, with their fine Gregorian plain chant; the perfection of their music is nearly flawless and the chaste and sober notes almost force the visiting tourist on his knees; and he would feel that the attitude of the tourists at Salzburg was impious and worldly. What it is that makes this chant sacred is hard to put into words, unless, of course, we look at its otherworldliness, its strangeness and its antiquity. But that would be archaism and indulgence in esthetic delicacies. Gregorian chant has been used officially not for these external reasons, accidental and passing, but for its inherent qualities. Its "canonization" does not mean that it is a model to be imitated but that it should inspire new forms, and develop in the spirit that created its immortal beauty. Its combination of clean sensuality and chaste spirituality, its ability to leave behind the individual personality without becoming cold musical mathematics, to cover the whole range of emotion from profound sadness to jubilant joy without ever descending into an animal groan or a bacchantic scream, makes it so "incarnational" that it seems to be the perfect robe for the mysteries of redemption by the incarnate God-Man. This chant—as also the other forms of chant, for example, Ambrosian, Toledan, and the varieties of Oriental chants—has an almost dogmatic correctness in its structure: it is true church music. Its structure is so strong that neither differences in interpretation nor reforms have been able to detract from its perfection to the ear of the average nonspecialist. The *"Christus factus est,"* the fifteenth Gloria, the Pentecost and Easter sequences, the *Communio* of Palm Sunday will always be perfect expressions of their content and mood.

But where do you hear such music? In cathedrals, convent chapels, and abbey churches on special occasions. There is no problem here for the pastoral clergy and their flock: only in few churches will such standards ever be achieved. It costs money, generations of training, a music-loving clergy, and other improbable prerequisites to achieve this. What we should discuss here is the condition we face in all countries of the globe in the parish. We must abstract from conditions that are not our own, from cathedrals and abbey churches, from so called genteel, upper-class and high-income parishes. We must look at the average parish we attend or serve, and we can see right away that between where we hear or say Mass and St. Meinrad's Abbey Church there is a chasm fixed that no mid-century Dives can cross—musically speaking.

In our sifting of aspects that complicate or even mislead, we should keep in mind one neat distinction: the esthetic approach and the pastoral one ought to be clearly separated in our minds. The ideal would be complete congruency of both. The pastor and his parishioners should be musically articulate and have good taste; the composer, the director, and the choir should think of the spiritual welfare and promotion of the Kingdom of God when they select and execute their music. But when the two yardsticks, esthetic and pastoral, clash, the esthetic will, in the raw condition of life, always yield.

But here again we must distinguish. The popular and simple in music should not always be designated the coarser, the more maudlin and sentimental: leadership here lies neither in the masses, in the smug low brow, nor in the untutored opinions of the musically illiterate. While the lilt of a tune may assure its popularity, more austere and reverent music may well be just as acceptable to a congregation that truly worships.

We should not confuse popularity with vulgarity, but at the same time we should not offer esoteric and recondite music fit only for the sophisticated, to the assembled brethren around the altar of the Lord.

A legalistic and moralistic mind is satisfied with a minimum: the silent presence of the congregation followed by maximum efficiency in dispatching the crowd. Whether this silence of the congregation is accompanied by the music of a performing choir makes little difference, as long as the congregation is silent and inactive. What the Holy Father proclaimed as the aim of all his reforms, a live participation and the spontaneous activity of all, is being nullified by such minimal practice all over the globe. It is not the music, neither its quality nor its quantity, that makes liturgy what it should be; the degrees of perfection in this matter are established by the dialogue, sung or spoken. That it always should bear the mark of dignity and good taste is integral, not essential. Pastorally and liturgically a poorly executed Mass in which all participate properly is preferable to the most perfect musical accompaniment, modern or ancient, chant or Stravinsky, where the congregation listens passively or becomes a mass of bored spectators. It may be extreme to point out that much of the effort now spent in the name of liturgy is actually a toilsome climb toward the wrong peak of liturgical heights; but again we are talking of parishes only. Sensitive and sophisticated ears may wince at the prospect of hearing the people's part sung not by a well trained choir, but by untrained and sometimes discordant voices around them. That is a price they will have to pay for being members of one Body, brothers and sisters of the musically "unwashed," in a congregation where the well dressed and educated lady may well sound much worse than the taxi driver behind her.

But then the parts of the Mass to be sung by the people are simple and not too long. Only the short responses, the Kyrie, the Gloria, the Credo, the Sanctus, and the Agnus Dei are to be sung and alternated with the choir. These are already available in simple settings, both in Gregorian chant as well as in simple modern versions modeled on chant. There is ample good and more complicated music for the choir and schola. We must keep in mind only that the people have a right and a duty to sing and the musicians an obligation to lead, without usurping, and to restrict their solo performances to the parts left for them. It will be the task of the choir, not only to perform good music but also to lead the singing of the congregation, to guide, to improve, and to correct. What is needed is patience, understanding, hard work, self-restricting modesty, a grasp of the subsidiary function of all participants, and the will to adjust to an apostolic task without sacrificing the high standards that are the ultimate aim. At a meeting of Church musicians in Paris in July, 1957, it was stated in clear terms "that according to the tradition of the Church Universal, at all times the part that belongs to the people must be safeguarded in the field of sacred music."

Tradition is not local custom, faulty, defective, and incomplete. Tradition is what is perfect, orthodox, and correct. Nobody should be so blind as to overlook the great problems and obstacles in the way of supplementing custom by tradition, but we cannot ignore it and refuse to act. Our eucharistic piety is now atomized, and the very teaching of the Church, that the end of this sacrament is the "building up" of the Church is, in practice, without expression. We should think of the communal aspects of the Last Supper and of the Apostolic Breaking of the Bread, but instead we are geared to the solitary mystical approach that excludes the brethren and the idea of the Church as Christ's Mystical Body.

When we discuss music in church, there is a certain confusion that must be cleared up. The highest worship of the great and mysterious God is silence, not only of the lips but also of the mind. This is as true for Christians as it was for Pythagoreans and other Greek philosophers, and as it is for Moslem mystics and for Indian sadhus. Jesus prayed alone on mountaintops, but he also instituted the Lord's Supper, which is after all what we mean by the Mass and liturgy. It is idle to argue which was closer to the Father, the silent communion in solitude or the mystery of the bread and wine. Both are necessary and are present in some form in all religions. The near-angelism, which ignores the full implications of the incarnation of Christ and by-passes the necessities of our bodily human nature, is really quite inhuman. "Catholic" is a term of many dimensions and depths; it signifies also the whole man as the object and subject of redemption. We cannot defend our silent congregrations; the use of bread, wine, water, and of words, the presence of their fellow baptized, clamor for lifting up their voices in common, especially when the liturgy protects the periods of silence and individual communion so amply and so firmly. And then one could go to church half an hour earlier or remain after Mass to taste the nearness of God in individual delight which is then made all the easier through the rich repast of Scripture gleaned from the central mystery.

Perhaps once the reforms now being worked out by the Holy See are introduced, and when the Mass is made more dramatic and self-explanatory by a clearer distinction of its parts and their function in the whole,* we may hope to see a greater adaptability of the rites and the music to the ability of modern congregations of "migratory city nomads." There is even hope that such parts as the entrance and Communion procession will be accompanied by vernacular hymns and psalms. The latter has been successfully tried

* Cf. H. A. Reinhold, *Bringing the Mass to the People*, Baltimore, 1960.

by the French Jesuit Père Gelineau and his famous English confrère Father Clifford Howell.

One must grasp the existential notion of worship. If we do not existentially, but only notionally, profess the Faith in the sacramental world, it will be impossible to grasp the necessity of visible and audible communal worship. So long as worship is not understood and accepted, music in church has lost its base. Singing demands more room for God in our souls, more space for our neighbor; or, as Guardini has expressed it, the Church awakened, become conscious, in our souls, The primal purpose of the sacrament, from which grew and blossomed what we today call the "Mass," is the "building up of the Church." It is ecclesial before it is individually mystical. As long as our teaching is late medieval and post-baroque, the ecclesial aspect of the Last Supper will always remain a dead letter and music will be regarded not as communal action but as an "occasional" embellishment of the service. The latest reforms of the Holy Sees are all animated and motivated by this concept, and it is therefore idle to argue about quality and quantity unless we have the exact meaning straight: music in church is not an expendable ornament for the esoteric and initiated, nor is it a pastime for the inarticulate and untutored; it is part of the mystery, even when it is reduced in awe and reverence to recitation in common.

6

The Eucharist and the Liturgy

A DANGEROUS INADEQUACY

The Holy Eucharist is a mystery in a twofold sense. It is a mystery of cult, that is, a re-presentation, a making present of the central fact of our salvation in a way which is unique in its reality. This reality is distinct from all other ways of being, *sui generis,* and therefore with St. Thomas we call it sacramental.

Since this sacramental "world entirely of its own" has no parallel in our world of experience and nature, the second meaning of the word "mystery," the more known one, now applies: the Eucharist is also an intellectual mystery, something which the human mind can never fully grasp even after its factual data have been revealed to man. We then know that we are, as it were, groping in the dark when we speak of it. We are taught that all we say is merely analogically true. Somehow our words are signposts showing the right direction and not more than that, since reality is as infinitely richer than our concepts and words, as is a living city over a signpost leading to it. There is, however, a true and rightful relation between our concept and the reality, and if we use the right terminology it really points toward live truth.

At the same time, the more we speculate about this mystery, the more we find the simple words of Christ and the liturgy adequate—more adequate than all other definitions or attempts at explanation with terms taken from natural philosophy and its theological derivatives. The faith of a child is here certainly greater than proud but inane intellectual attempts to understand a strictly supernatural mystery. There are the plain original things, words and actions: bread, wine, the altar table; the plain unmistakable words of Christ: body, blood; the separation of both and the allusion to death and sacrifice in the words of His institution, and finally His gestures of blessing, breaking, looking up to the Father. Professional theology will go further, probably has to go further! But what about faith, which is built on the very person of Christ, His infallible Church and the supernatural factor of grace, for which we cannot account by experience?

The divine world approaches us here as in all sacraments and in the Church herself by way of the senses; it strikes our eyes, ears, our sensory faculties, our palate, and our nostrils. For those who accept the Incarnation and the miracles of Christ there is nothing to be surprised at in seeing the unapproachable, distant God convey His life to us through the symbols of matter.

Since Christ instituted His sacraments as symbols, they share the character of all symbols: they signify and indicate something. A light, painted or actual, is an apt means of indicating and signifying enlightenment and truth. The pouring of water over an object aptly symbolizes its cleansing. (Nobody would ever imagine that ink or paint are suited to symbolize the cleansing of the soul in baptism.) We should respect the good and simple things that their Creator and the Institutor of the sacraments has stamped with the divine seal of His approval. Because of theological speculations, which are in themselves entirely correct and legitimate on the basis of history and tradition, we have, however, almost lost sight of symbols, so that we are engrossed with secondary and deductive truths. In the case of many theologians, I say, it looks as if the deduced doctrine of natural concomitance in the Holy Eucharist has served to obscure the first and greater things, those which are comprised under the term "*vis verborum,*" the primary realities immediately visible: the divine Food, the Sacrifice.

Now, what is this all about. And is it important?

It is certainly important, because it is the function of the liturgical texts to conserve the primary emphases in spite of the many
theological and popular tendencies to wander away from Christ's
and His Church's originality. One glance through our popular
prayer and sermon books and even some theological literature
proves how widespread these tendencies have become. They even
affect the very interpretation of liturgical texts and succeed in mis-
leading men who want to advocate a return to liturgy. E. I. Watkin
suggests in his *Catholic Centre* that the Divine Office should continually be chanted before the Blessed Sacrament exposed. That is
not only against all liturgical common sense and tradition, but
even against normal liturgical legislation, which forbids the Blessed
Sacrament to be reserved on choir altars in cathedrals and abbey
churches and makes the contrary an exception. Here the secondary
has obviously superseded the primary, the derivative the original.
The Divine Office is not directed to the Real Presence, but to the
Father in heaven; and that is a very important difference, and not
just quibbling.

If men do not start their sermons and meditations with the
primary facts but with deductions from them, they simply get a
wrong start and wander in that mysterious region between visible
and supernatural reality, between the "signpost" and the thing. It is
at least indelicate and shows lack of good theological taste to emphasize through the whole length of a sermon that the priest has
the power of "locking Jesus up" in the tabernacle, of "carrying Him
in his arms," of denying Him to the people or of giving Him to them,
making Him depend on the will of His priest, and other pious vul-
garities. This can only happen if and when the emphasis has shifted
from the primary content of the sacrament to secondary aspects and
deductions. It is perhaps through our legitimate defense of Christ's
Real Presence against heretics that we have to such a large extent
lost the liturgical and active attitude toward the Blessed Sacrament
and have acquired instead a sort of intellectual and quietistic contemplation of concomitant facts.

Anyone reading the three last prayers before Holy Communion in our Mass will admit that they are directed toward Christ and not toward the Blessed Sacrament. Let us bluntly say it: for the liturgy and its purpose there is never a total identification of the Sacrament and Christ in His glory. It simply disregards the concomitance because the latter would make a real understanding of the liturgical action impossible. If we dwell on the fact that the Real Presence of Christ's body and blood logically also implies the presence of the Whole Christ under each of the species—which is obviously so for our speculative purposes—the Mass becomes an insoluble problem and consists in nothing but the drawing of Christ to earth to make Him "rule the world from the tabernacle" or to be "consoled there in His dark and lonely abode" by pious souls. That is actually the predominant idea in many minds. Then there arise almost naturally such theological atrocities and liturgical misfits as Kleutgen's theory that Christ's sacrifice in the Mass consists in His giving up His heavenly throne to dwell in a little piece of bread; the Mass becomes a moral "sacrifice" of self-humiliation, and liturgy and theology are blasted to bits with the dynamite of emotional sentimentality. The analogical character of all we can rightfully say about this Great Mystery—in both senses—has in such cases been forgotten, and authors tread the delicious pastures of unrevealed divine mystery with their hobnailed boots of triviality.

Some apparently unimportant innovations that radically affected Eucharistic piety took place in the early Middle Ages. One of them was the introduction of the use of unleavened bread for Mass in the eighth century. This was a departure not only from a very old tradition, but a departure from the practice of the Eastern Churches then still in union with Rome. It would be about the same thing as if, let us say, the United States would rescind the legislation of Gregory VII about the celibacy of priests while the rest of the Church maintained the now eight-hundred-year-old law. We can see that the thin white wafer of our present-day hosts has very little in common with the ordinary bread, rolls, and loaves we eat in our homes and hotels. To the naïve mind these hosts, even un-consecrated, somehow look mysterious, angelic, spiritual in their frail whiteness.

It is easier too to expose our kind of host in a monstrance, and it melts easily on the tongue.

About the same time that the wafer was introduced, the neglect which the average Catholic showed for the other species of the Blessed Sacrament had gone so far in the Middle Ages that councils in France had to remind the priests that they were obliged to lift the chalice as well as the host at the Consecration, and that they were not supposed to hold the host up unusually long, to wave it about, or to bless the people with it at that moment. Even the intro-duction of the Feast of the Most Precious Blood and its elevation to a higher rank under Pope Pius XI has not changed visibly the aloofness of the faithful (and priests?) toward this species. If the Church saw fit to prescribe the use of the chalice for the faithful she could do so any day. Its use was not altogether dead even as late as the fifteenth century. It may be that it received its deathblow from the unruly, rebellious, and heretical reformers of the late Middle Ages who made a matter of discipline into a matter of faith.

In both cases the departure from immemorial tradition, common usage, and the apparent contradiction to the letter of the law were based on reasons of convenience. The change was not decreed, but followed a gradual introduction or a new custom which had with-stood all efforts of the authorities to uphold the old tradition. We know how bitter the East was about the matter and how she raised the cry of heresy. Nearly all Eastern branches of the Church were living in a state of siege, oppressed by despots or Moslems. We can understand how, as a consequence, they felt all the more obliged to preserve their precious spiritual heritage by a strict and rigid preservation of its outward form.

This greater freedom of development, however, which kept the Church in the West in closer contact with the trend of spiritual and intellectual movements and, in a way, with popular piety, has had its drawbacks. Yet I wonder if the claim of the Eastern Churches, that they have kept their people closer to the liturgy than the "Romans" with their "para- and pseudo-liturgical substitutes," is true. Eastern liturgy is fine, and usually carried out with grandeur. But it never seemed to me in my practical experience of the several Orthodox liturgies I have attended on three continents that the people really took part or understood very much. Their participation through reception of the sacrificial Victim is certainly not as frequent as in the Latin rite. So if the East reproaches us that we disregard Christ's second summons of "drinking," we can justly reply that we seem to be more anxious to obey Him by frequent "eating."

But with all our nearness to the people and with the greater freedom of mystics, theologians, and popular currents to influence our practical liturgy in its broadest and most extended sense, we must admit that we have suffered too. Not in dogma or in morals, but in practice. The popular mind tends toward isolation of individual traits. Aided by the above-mentioned convenient changes and tremendously impelled by counteraction against heresy and misrepresentation, we have now come so far that the whole emphasis has been changed from the center of the mystery to its periphery, especially in extraliturgical practice and in the ascetic and mystic literature of the day. The Real Presence is the thing that impresses our popular piety. The person of Christ in its static values, His humanity in its historical aspects, and sometimes a bold disregard of what St. Thomas said so clearly, that Christ is in the sacrament *non tamquam in loco, sed tamquam in sacramento,* not as in a place but as in a sacrament—all these are the things above the surface of our Eucharistic consciousness, while the real foreground facts have sunk down to the bottom of professional theological books and official statements of doctrine.

Of course we are happily inconsistent, or else how could we see a priest using the Blessed Sacrament for benediction without feeling that our slightly overemphasized "personalistic" idea receives a great shock? Few people seem to realize that there is any approach to the glorified Lord other than through the tabernacle door. The simplicity and the lucidity which the Blessed Sacrament carries in its original institution and in our liturgy has yielded in popular minds to an elaborate system of conclusions which it was right to make but which shifted the emphasis from the foreground to the background. This does not always mean greater profundity.

Here, too, the liturgical movement should not destroy. The shift of emphasis has not helped us too much. But the opposite attitude of the East has not helped them either. A better understanding of ourselves will lead to a sane middle way which will do justice to the facts as given by Christ and also to our tradition, now seven hundred years old.

FAMILY COMMUNION

Without relying on early Marxist theory but just as efficiently, perhaps even more efficiently, modern capitalist society has had a practical effect on the family which looks like the fulfillment of the communist dream. The family is going to pieces. Those things which preserved the natural family in the past are fast disappearing, for example, the economic community which the family once formed on farms, among craftsmen, in small establishments. Father, mother, and children worked in and for the family, which embraced sometimes two or more generations. But in our time the home is beginning to resemble a boardinghouse in which the boarders are relatives who seem to like each other and who may even pool their incomes. I don't know how much farms have been affected in this way, but in cities, where father and mother and growing-up children work in different places and meet irregularly, there is certainly little of the old natural family left. I don't say that all families are like that or have reached the extreme of the boardinghouse type. But comparing families of today with those of one or two generations back, we certainly cannot fail to see in which direction the wind is blowing. All the little straws fly the same way.

The greater part of education is being shifted to the school. Religion is becoming a private affair that concerns individuals and the clergy. Amusement is sought in clubs, bars, movies, roadhouses, in the out-of-doors, not with family members but with a boy friend, a girl friend, or some other friend. Even illness and infirmity are gently removed from the family circle and shifted to public agencies like hospitals, clinics, and other community services. With mounting divorce ratio the disintegrating family is on the march. Maybe this also is exaggerated, but again there are those little straws that all fly in just one direction.

What are we going to do about it? We cannot simply tell our young men and women: "Look at Nazareth; that is your ideal." If they are good people they will say, "Yes, Father, but how?" We have no details of how family life went on in Nazareth. We know only that the Son of God was infinitely more perfect as a son of His earthly parents than we could hope to be, and similarly, in a finite way, was Our Lady as a mother and St. Joseph as a foster father. If some post-medieval writers have painted us family idyls of Nazareth that grew on the soil of their Western European and "bourgeois" imagination, fastened to the ground of revealed truth by the thin pegs of four or five not very precise quotations from the New Testament, they have given us a picture more of their own time and mind than of something for moderns to imitate.

It is not the doctrine of the Church that is at stake. We know what that is. We have Leo XIII's and Pius XI's great encyclicals on Christian marriage (not on family life). "The father the head, the mother the heart"—a great and wonderful statement. But this statement has to participate in the constant process of "Incarnation" that began when the *Word* became flesh in a stable in a little Jewish town. It became flesh so completely that it had to work miracles and rise from the dead to be recognized as the Word. These great truths cry constantly for new forms of realization.

I think this is a warning to us. Let us not insist too much on old forms and traditions of family life. Let us rather try to rebuild the family on a supernatural basis, and demonstrate its essentials. Every family is an *ecclesiola,* a miniature Church. And the Church realizes Herself in Her supreme idea at the altar, in the Holy Eucharist.

The process of reeducation has to start not with the children but with our priests first of all, and secondly with our teachers, thirdly with our organizations, and fourthly with our actual and prospective fathers and mothers. If we bring it about that father and mother receive Communion with and at the same time as their children, a hundred other things will naturally follow. It will act like the sudden rise of a contrary wind, which at first will whirl the aforementioned straws into confusion but soon will send them all flying in the right direction against the tendency to dissolution and anarchy. Just imagine what this embraces: the family a community of prayer and sacrament in church. This cannot fail to influence the home. It will build new responsibilities, it will make fathers and mothers eager to help their little ones prepare. They will go to confession together.

Still, there is that "confused mess" of transition! What about discipline: Holy Name men, sodality girls, Knights, Catholic Daughters, St. So-and-So Guild, school girls and boys, Scouts in their different pews, coming up together, countable, orderly, like a sacred team. It is so much more reassuring. It has always been this way. . . . You see why I started with the reeducation of the clergy and the teachers, and why I mentioned the organizations before the real objects of all this, the parents? In some parishes this will be as revolutionary as the storming of the Winter Palace in Petrograd, 1917.

Finally, what about our indulgenced Communions in a body? Are we going to lose all those graces? I shall not answer this question, but shall ask a few of my own: Why were those indulgences given, at what time? Are those reasons now more important than the reasons for family Communion? And if we don't want to lose indulgences, can we not get indulgences for corporate family Communion from the same Holy See that is so concerned with the restoration of our families that two popes within forty years wrote worldwide encyclicals, and another one changed the recently reformed calendar of his predecessor back to its old "unliturgical" character for the sake solely of restoring the ideal of the Christian family among the faithful? Is it perhaps our human fear of the uncertain, of commotion, of change, of trouble and effort that persuades us that we cannot do it? Tell me, is there any doubt that, once we have tried to rebuild the center of the family, the outgrowth will be a new, true Catholic family pattern of life flowing from the altar?

7

A Few Reforms

VERNACULAR IN THE LITURGY

A very serious problem of many Catholics is their spiritual inarticulateness and helplessness. Our treasury of prayer has been reduced to four or five formulas, which although in themselves excellent are in danger of becoming units of spiritual "performance." All that is done with congregations or individuals is to urge them to repeat one or two accepted formulas and to produce greater emphasis by greater quantity, by having them recite ten "Our Fathers" and "Hail Marys" instead of five, and so on. Thus whole aspects of prayer have become so shrunken and crippled through inactivity that even the praise of God in the "Glory be to the Father" is usually just a tag for other prayers of petition. How it would widen and exercise the soul, fill it with lifeblood and fresh spiritual air, if it could expand in the great rhythms of the *Gloria in Excelsis* (in the vernacular of course), in the *Te Deum,* the *Te Decet Laus,* the psalms and hymns of our liturgy! What vast spiritual wealth this would open up to our modern Catholics! And the resultant difference of volume and tone color would be like that between a small mouth harmonica and a booming organ in all its richness.

If the vernacular were used, there would be no sense to reading it off "by oneself," but the priest would have to read it to the people and the people would have to understand it, because they would again come to listen, to respond, to walk in procession, and not to read out of books—except for hymns and psalms. There are dozens of reasons that clamor for a vernacular liturgy, and let us hope that this clamor becomes a habit of all devout Catholics of the English tongue until it will be the *vox populi,* which is the *vox Dei.*

For my part, I am convinced that none of the adversaries of the movement for the vernacular has enough to say to defeat it. Will the hierarchy be won? I am quite sure that many bishops are already won, even though their position and their grave responsibilities do not allow them to side with any movement. Their task is to protect tradition and to watch for dangerous trends. Thus their attitude is naturally one of caution and reserve. Will Rome give in? Don Luigi Sturzo once wrote to me that in Italy *vernacular* means a different version in every province. I must confirm that: Sicilian is not Italian, nor is Venetian or Piedmontese. Italian is a *"koine,"* a *lingua franca* of the literati and almost as strange as Latin. It is too cultured for the average man to speak. But that did not prevent fascist agitators, newspapers and organizers from being understood. And if we admit that even the vernacular does not mean the "colloquial" language, we have found the right medium. If Rome has a guarantee that liturgical English will be noble and sacred, not pompous, not pietistic, no "religious cliché" English, I suppose Rome will be satisfied. Am I, of all people, speaking for Rome? No, but I can point out that the Croats have the Roman Mass in Slavonic, and the Czechs more than thirty years ago received permission to have their patrons' festival Masses in Czech. And more than that: the Rumanians of the Eastern Rite who are in union with us have their rite in modern Rumanian, which is constantly being revised to bring it up to date. I don't think Anglo-Saxon Catholicity and loyalty to the Holy See can be called more questionable than that of these nations! Moreover, most advocates of the vernacular advocate leaving a token part of the liturgy in Latin, that part which is the hardest to translate and is strictly the priest's prayer: from the Preface (or Offertory prayers) to the Amen before the *Pater Noster.*

Older schoolbooks emphasized the symbolic value of Latin as a bond of unity and the fact that a Catholic might go anywhere and find himself at home with the same Latin Mass. I have always marveled that this argument was swallowed so easily and so unquestioningly. In the first place: Are the Eastern Christians with their different liturgy plus their different languages for that reason lesser Catholics, or in a lesser union with the center of Catholic life? Are they a sort of *"pars minus honesta"* (less respectable members) of Christ's Body, the Church? Latin liturgy in its Roman form would only symbolize the unity of that part of the Church that happens to have the Roman Mass, and this for purely historical reasons, in most cases. What of Milan, Toledo, Braga, Lyons? Is there anything wrong with our Dominicans, Carthusians and Cistercians? Quite apart from the inconclusiveness of this argument that contradicts facts, dogma, charity and justice, I think the people who use it confuse unity with uniformity. And I don't like the latter at all. I don't think Anglo-Saxons like it either. Even Rome, I am confident, does not like it, although her enemies accuse her of a clandestine love for it.

And then that other reason: "The same Latin Mass wherever you go." Even if this were the case, it would be all right if you knew Latin; but what help is it to you if you don't? If you do go to Germany or Poland or Egypt or some other foreign country, what is more likely: that you learn Latin or the language of the country? The answer is obvious. As long as it is the same Mass, what difference does it make if the prayers and readings are in the vernacular, since Latin is only theoretically, alas! our mother tongue.

With all this I still look forward with fear and trembling to the "translation." Look at our different versions of the Bible. The most beautiful one is not ours; Douay is admittedly poor, and the new Version does not seem to find universal approval. "Woman, what is that to Me and to thee? My hour is not yet come," was what we read in Greek, Latin, and English hitherto. It makes sense, its context is clear, and the problem it creates is neither undogmatic nor irreverent to Our Lord nor to Our Lady. Now we have it smoothed out: "What wouldst thou have Me do, woman?"—and all for the sake of sparing our "feelings" concerning Our Lady, even though the following words make no sense any more. Wasn't Christ entitled to teach Our Lady, to correct her understanding, and then to yield to His mother, to give her that "untimely" miracle she asked for? Now, if this kind of thing is going to happen to our liturgy—what a pity!

It is not only what and how much of it we want in the vernacular; the "how" of it is also important. Nobody questions the quality of Cardinal Newman's English, its elegance and its richness. And yet, just compare the fresh, lapidary vigor of the hymn *Creator alme siderum* with his version. Of the *"Te deprecamur hagie venture iudex saeculi"* he made: "Thou too shalt be our judge at length," and so on. It is one step more in the direction that was fatally taken under Urban VIII and that gave us our present watered-down, "fluent" hymns. Gone is *"sobria ebrietas."* *"Urbs Hierusalem beata,"* and what do we have instead? Slick, moralistic, elegant versifications. Who will guarantee us that the Roman part of the missal (collects, prefaces)—not the scriptural part alone—will retain its vigor, its precision, its virility, its *cursus* (so that we won't stammer and stutter), and its chaste reverence? Our popular prayers certainly are enough to arouse fearsome forebodings!

And then there will be the question of what to do with the psalmodic parts of the Mass. These are taken from the psalter current before St. Jerome's revision. They have been retained even after the revision, because their wording makes liturgical sense, is full of allusions, responses, symbolic meanings. They harmonize with the lessons, the mystery celebrated, the collects, the antiphons. Is all this wonder and miracle, this beautiful subtlety, this deep symbolism to go by the board? What a pity, and what an impoverishment! Great harm was done in the Middle Ages by the mutilations of the Offertory song, the amputation of the Introit psalm and the entire disappearance of the psalm that puts the Communion antiphon into its proper and meaningful relief. Shall this great thing be further vulgarized, platitudinized, sentimentalized, subjectivized? Let us hope not. Or shall we just sing a hymn instead, being unsubtle Nordics? Our Catholic hymns, in almost all languages, are deplorable. To take from the rich heritage of Anglicans and Lutherans—although the majority of their hymns are translations from the liturgy—would hurt our pride.

What I am personally afraid of in the solution of these grave problems is a "commission" of professors who know all about their fields but do not speak the language of the people, or the saints, or the poets, or whose spirituality is and has been fed on an individualistic, subjective diet, who will smooth over, streamline, modernize, make more dogmatic, less shocking, more elegant, less uneven, what they find. And then we shall be stuck with it. And that would be worse than what we have now, because it would falsify the spirit of our Roman liturgy. There is hope, of course, that a second Pius X will come and finish the task of clearing the weeds. If, however, what the martyrs, the Fathers and Popes created will once have been watered down in its entirety to our bourgeois mentality and speech, the damage may prove grave—and permanent.

And yet, we cannot afford to lose time. Michael de la Bedoyère has in the past told us how serious all of this is. *Religio depopulata*— a Church without people—is a terrible prospect. Our growing generation may not be willing to listen to us who failed them twice and left them to die and bleed for us and our disorganized world, born of materialism, smugness, and selfishness. But they will listen to Christ, living in His mysteries. Can they, if they do not even understand His words?

Let us then make the issue of English in our liturgy clear. It is not, in the view of liturgists on either side of the Atlantic, a wholesale translation of the liturgy into modern colloquial English. I do not think that such a course was ever advocated here or in England. We have always been careful not to say: the liturgy in vernacular, but to say: vernacular in the liturgy. When we say this, we never advocate a "new liturgy" either. I, for my part, am horrified at such a prospect, when I look at the "liturgical" productions of the last hundred years, in and out of the missal. They have about as much resemblance to the genuine thing as a neo-Gothic parish church to

Chartres. And if I think of our "production" in novenas and prayer books, I am quite certain that anything beyond a good translation would be murder. What is in question is only a good, the best possible, translation of those parts of the liturgy that we think ought to be translated.

Which are the parts we think ought to be translated? Why translate them again when we have already a score of passable translations?

To answer the second question first: because none of the existing translations is sufficient. Because none of them was made, corrected, and authorized by the only institution that can do it in a way that everybody will accept: the Church Herself, in this particular case the hierarchies of the English-speaking world. The English must be the best available and on the level of a T. S. Eliot or W. H. Auden. Its savor must be akin to Winston Churchill's power of formulation and must have, on a religious plane, the earthiness and force which he shows in his political language. It must be done by men sufficiently scholars of Scripture, liturgics, and history to be able to take a word like "mystery," which has a definite liturgical meaning, and render it so as to bring out this meaning in a way every man can grasp. This is neither a field for well-meaning little stylists, second-rate poets and would-be mystics, nor for the scribes whose world consists in jots and tittles over which they stumble in awkward contortions. No translation is better than the wrong one. We shall have to wait—even if, in my opinion, it is five minutes before closing time.

The parts that I think should be translated are those that concern the people. In other words, I would not touch a single Latin line meant for silent recitation by the priest as long as the rubrics require such silent recitation. Since the people cannot hear it anyway, why stir up endless controversy about the correct translation of texts that are extremely hard to render in English and that involve all sorts of dogmatic and historical issues over which professors have fought inconclusive wars for centuries? Besides, if Latin is in a way a symbolic bond of unity for the Western part of our Church, this is a part where it does not interfere with popular participation. It also will satisfy, at least partly, those who claim that the "mystery character" of the liturgy is best preserved by the use of a solemn, dead, obsolete, and "sacred" language. The canon of the Mass is what makes the Mass a "mystery" in the word's dogmatic and liturgical sense. Therefore, while I do not admit that their reasoning is right at all, why not spare their feelings by leaving at least this part in the venerable, universal tongue of ecclesiastical officialdom? It will not rob the people of anything anyway, as long as the canon remains secret.

This leaves us with an English rendering of all the parts the people hear, or sing themselves once they have wrested their rightful property out of the hands of choirs and professional singers who have taken over their part. I want the Gospel, the Epistle, the Collect and Post-Communion, the processional anthems (Introit, Offertory, and Communion—all plus their psalms), the Our Father, the Preface, the Gloria, Kyrie, Sanctus, and Agnus Dei, and, above all, the responses in English. I would be willing to make another concession at the Nicene Creed, as its content, once translated, is easy to remember, and to sing it in Latin satisfies our friends who claim that Latin is the symbol of unity. Above all, it is an official formula, not a hymn or prayer like the rest, in spite of the fact that many a choir performs it like an oratorio. Its flavor is juridical, in the word's best sense, and its delight comes to him who rejoices in lucid and crystalline dogmatic formulations as others revel in lyrics. Such people are few and far between. However, I would be able to see many good reasons to translate it too.

No doubt, many difficulties arise. But these difficulties do not arise from the rendering in English. They are already there and only invisible now because the whole thing is a clouded issue to the people. Take our present Introit: the choir sings one psalm while the priest and his closer assistants recite another one at the foot of the altar and then, when the choir is already busy with the Kyrie, the priest proceeds to read again by himself what the choir has just finished. The translation will bring this situation out into the open, and it will have to be decided if these sacerdotal prayers are part of the private preparation of the priest or are not, and whether the Introit is still a processional or just a relic of bygone times dutifully performed because a rigid tradition prescribes it. All this will come to life when translated and taken out of the esoteric atmosphere in which the people now hold it.

It is quite natural that the advocacy of such a change—which affects neither faith nor morals nor even discipline—comes as a bold endeavor in an age that values monolithic uniformity above the practice of speaking your mind and playing the role of the self-appointed prophet. There is a great deal to be said against these efforts, their timeliness, their feasibility, and their eventual hope of achieving anything but futile and angry controversy, so let us look at the opposition. (I am not discussing the possibility of seeing the whole discussion cut short by an order of the competent authorities. If that happens, a Catholic has only one answer—obedience.)

There are those who feel that vernacular usage has unsavory connotations—Cranmer, Luther, eighteenth century rationalism, and weak-kneed concessions to and aping of Protestantism. It is the curse of these precedents that makes change so difficult. While it is a historic fact that these dissenters and rebels introduced their vernacular forms of worship as a consequence of departure, and that there seems to be no case of the opposite procedure, the opponents of English in the liturgy refuse to look at it that way and prefer to see in the desire for vernacular the symptoms of rebellion. This is no surprise in a generation that has been educated preponderantly to an anti-Protestant outlook. You can't live fenced in a sort of ghetto without acquiring an aggressive apologetic and negative attitude. A siege, especially after a retreat, will give you a feeling of inferiority that cannot be argued away; it must be outgrown.

We can point to another line of precedents whose most noble representatives are Sts. Cyril and Methodius. When they translated the liturgy into Slavonic, they too were reported to Rome, but were acquitted and encouraged by the Holy See. Or we can point out that Rome herself changed from the original Greek to Latin at a time when Latin was still the "vernacular" in Rome. That no Celtic or Teutonic Cyrils or Methodiuses arose to do the North the favor the East was receiving two hundred years later has cultural and political causes, and to investigate them here would be out of the question. Had it not been for the rebellion of the sixteenth century and the bad odor into which such attempts were brought forever after, we might have had our vernacular long ago. The Mediterranean countries are close in language to their Latin liturgy. Only the Celtic, Teutonic, and West Slavic nations—aside from the missions—assist at the instructions, hymns, and prayers without being able to make them the language of their heart and mind as well as of their ears and tongues.

A great deal has been made of the word "mystery." Leading minds of the liturgical movement have claimed that the sacred mysteries ought not to be brought out into the market places of the world on the same level with TV, radio, and revival services. They have pointed to the difference between church and other architecture. Even vestments have been used as an argument against the vernacular in the sanctuary. This seems to me a forest of fallacies. Mystery and mysteriousness are not the same thing. The announcement of the Epistle and Gospel is for the people. That requires that the people know what I announce. Mysteriousness is where it belongs—during the canon. The vesting of the priest in sacerdotal garments lifts him out of the purely human sphere and submerges his individuality in something super-personal—but it is no disguise; it does not make him "mysterious." Besides, words are signs conveying ideas, if anything. Only men like Talleyrand thought that words were means to hide thought. Thus to claim that the mysteriousness of the mystery needs an unknown tongue is one of the weakest arguments one can use.

As far as architecture is concerned, the people who built Romanesque churches built also Romanesque warehouses and dwellings—not Egyptian pyramids or Attic temples. There may be scores of arguments against the vernacular in the sanctuary, but this is a poor one.

But one of the worst reasons for excluding the vernacular from our liturgy is the argument of cultural preservation. European intellectuals visualize with horror an America in which the last vestige of Hellenic antiquity will be gone. And they see in the future American Church something degraded to the level of a sect, something plebeian to a terrible degree, something devoid of all those Latin graces that have survived the onslaught of modern totalitarian, egalitarian commercialism, and excessive emotionalism only in the Roman Church. But it is not the task of Christ's mysteries to embalm or preserve Hellenic or Roman or any civilization, but to pour out grace and to bring about the realization of the Mystical Body of the Lord. If this can be achieved more easily by cutting out an unnecessary detour, let us advocate it.

This has nothing to do with personal preferences. With Father C. C. Martindale I say that it will be a sad day for me when I cannot hear my voice at the altar recite the beautiful and familiar Latin. I fear and tremble when I think of all the possibilities of a hasty, incompetent translation. I know that immeasurable values and worlds of connotations will be lost even in a masterly translation. But who shares my grief? Not one per cent of my people. They do not ask for translation. As a matter of fact, they may be opposed to it, considering the education they have had, the ignorance in which they live as to the beauty of it all, and the aversion to any change in what seems to them unchanged since Christ's day. I realize all this. I realize also that no one in authority can shoulder the responsibility by himself of inaugurating such a change. It will take years of unofficial discussion, years of careful research, great care and caution in the choice of translators and translations, in the preparation of the people. It may be altogether too difficult to perform. Shall we dismiss it, then, without examining its merits? I do not think so.

The specter of the *Religio Depopulata* is before us, even though we are one of the few nations where this specter is still dim. That this should become a reality is unthinkable, and to prevent it a certain periodical contraction toward vital essentials is needed. What better way than by teaching God's people an immediate living in His Son's holy mysteries.

NOTES ON A BREVIARY REFORM

Most priests who have talked to me during these last years have suggested a rather simple method of reforming the breviary: translate it into the vernacular, shorten it, take out the lessons that either are too legendary or incomprehensible and a few other more or less simple desiderata. To have to read year after year how St. Augustine allegorizes on the thirty-eight-year-old lame man at the pool of Bethesda, or to take with a straight face his excuse for Jacob's fraud as not being "a lie, but a mystery," is not only taxing modern frankness and sense of proportion, but it reflects on the whole Office as something with whose honesty one can trifle and whose value as a nourishment of souls can be doubted. Therefore a few features have been emphasized: "cleaning up" the second (historical) nocturn of the night office; translation; more scriptural readings in longer contexts without chopping them up as is the rule now, spreading the psalms over two or even four weeks instead of one, and so on.

The opponents of such a reform, few as they are, claim that the individual cleric does not have to read the breviary as he would read a meditation: he reads it as a member of the Church, joining the innumerable choirs of men and angels. They find nothing incongruous in the silent reader answering himself, for example, *Dominus vobiscum*, they visualize themselves as the Church praying and praising. This is the official sort of answers one gets, when questioning the value of the breviary for the pastoral section of the clergy. What happens usually is that the hard-working and the less strenuously occupied read their office before they retire, sleepy and drained of all concentration, to get it over with. As their prayer life is centered around meditation, examination of conscience, visits to the tabernacle, rosary, and Stations of the Cross as solid bases of their spirituality, they are fed to satiety, and the Office comes in as a cross to be borne in obedience—which of course has its reward.

This is an attitude which seems to me to be indefensible: the Office not only consists of Holy Scripture, but of writings of the great Fathers and Doctors of the Church, the gems of Christian hymnody, a web of profoundly conceived antiphons and responsories, all assembled with great unction, subtlety, and masterful poetic sense. How can we assign such a Cinderella role to one of the greatest prayers ever composed by man? The Office is also intertwined with the great mystery of every day, the Mass. It supposedly sets the seasonal mood of our spiritual year—provided we take time to savor it sufficiently—if we have the time and energy left to do so. One might say that a well said Office forces the cleric to reestablish a rhythm of life that is more priestly then the hustle and bustle of so many pastoral lives and that therefore we should reform the clergy instead of laying hands on the heritage of a millennium. The reformers with a backward glance at the perfect period of the past miss only one thing in their cogent reasoning, and that is that you can't turn the clock back and that we are all moving in the opposite direction, either reluctantly or willingly: the momentum is there for all to see.

If the conservatives are not right, the superficial reformers with scissors and paste are even more to be questioned.

We have to keep in mind that our Office, as we say it now, is a monk's solemn choir Office round the clock, night and day, which was given to the parish clergy around the time of the great reformers like Gregory VII. "Every priest a monk" seems to have been his and the other reformers' motto. Under him celibacy was made a law for all major clerics, and the monastic prayer of the hours was made obligatory for all the tonsured, with little regard for their isolation and less for their working hours: they were to sing and chant their night Office; before dawn they were to welcome the great symbol of Christ's Resurrection, the sun, with the chanting of Lauds; before the work of the day started they had to acquit themselves of the dedication of their day's work in the Office of Prime.

At nine, and noon, and at nones the day was to be reconsecrated and the memory of the sacred mystery had to be enlivened by Tierce, Sext, and None: truly a great spiritual scheme of a consecrated working day, unsurpassed by later devotions of more "subjective" inspiration. When the day was sinking the Magnificat of the great Vesper chant bade farewell to the departing sun as a symbol of the Lord. Finally the cleric was to retire with Simeon's parting words on his lips, embedded in the great Compline services, followed by deep silence with nothing but God and eternity on his mind. A whole day was thus lifted out of its pure and unconsecrated drabness and earthiness: incense seemed to rise from fields being plowed, from smithies, from printing shops, kitchens and nurseries and hospitals and even the stock exchanges. Could there be a more Christian and godly pattern of life? In this pattern Christ "through his most gentle Advent had indeed come to consecrate the world" (Martyrology, Dec. 24, Office of Prime). This was almost a life lived like music, the Kingdom of God on earth, if you add that all was charity and justice to boot and purity reigned supreme wherever the monks found a willing people and cleric to adopt this monastic way beyond the gate of the monastery and in the bosom of the families and in the market places of the cities.

The sad thing is that this never existed, and what existed of it— a shadow of the great vision—was destroyed by the very Christians that practiced it. Long before the Reformation the wick had burned down and flickered faintly before drowning. But we must pray and do so in common and with order and a consecratory effect on our souls and on our institutions as well. The gate of the never-never-land paradise is closed and its way of life has now become a half-understood burden with little or no effect on those who practice it in dogged obedience, who when athirst in their souls go to shallower wells dug in despair of making the deeper wells yield water for famished souls that battle the cruel rhythms of the Industrial Age, our age.

Without romantic nostalgia and vain attempts to restore what sank in the ocean of time forever—not even Cluny lasted more than a century, in spite of its separation from the business of the world—what do I propose to do? I think we should keep what can be kept and prune away what is impossible to realize in a modern pastoral priest's or missionary's life.

We should not only preserve the Scripture, but have more of it circumspectly and intelligently selected, distributed over enough time so that all can be read with attention even by busy clerics, let us say in the course of three or four years. Legends and historical biographies should be treated as such, because legends are in a subtle way history: they are the crystallization of the saints' impact on the ruder minds.

The division of the Office over the day should take account of the twentieth century rhythm of life: outside of severe monasteries nobody will stir from his fitful sleep at midnight or before sunup. Therefore what is now Matins and Lauds, consolidated into one twenty-minute reading prayer, should be thus arranged that it takes the place of morning prayer and meditation. A short Prime should be a thanksgiving after Mass and a dedication of the day's work. Of the three little hours a midday Sext should be recited by heart—a psalm, hymn, chapter and the Lord's Prayer. A fifteen-minute prayer should combine Vespers and Compline before retiring. The recommended devotions and the practice of walking in the presence of God, conscience alert and mind lifted from the pedestrian details of daily life, would by itself be a great help to lead consecrated lives, without the burden of sterile performances, imposed and half resented. Morning, after Mass, noon and evening Office should be sufficient: what is lost in quantity is easily gained in quality. At least all clerics of good will would have a chance to be spiritual men—the grace of their Office giving them strength to do less, better.

The greatest problem, as I see it now, is the use of the psalms. It is an ill understood loyalty to the sacred Scriptures to evaluate them all alike as masterpieces of their kind. Surely nobody in his right mind will maintain that "The Lord is my shepherd," "Out of the depths have I cried to thee," and "By the rivers of Babylon"—three masterpieces—are matched by Psalms 55 or 108, or by one of the dry historical recountings of the past of Israel. Nor is there any match within the body of the psalter for the Miserere or Psalm 119. Who does not get rightfully bored to distraction by the interminable and repetitious—and a bit pharisaic—Psalm 118 which now lies in wait for the tired pastor—on, of all days, Sunday.

In the first place we modern men can't get accustomed to the idea of saying more than one psalm at a time, especially not a collection that are fitted together more by length than by their contents. There is a glut of psalms that causes indigestion in our present Matins, Lauds, and Vespers above all, but the other canonical hours are by no means free from overcrowding. The desert Fathers believed in quantity; they said all one hundred and fifty psalms every day, as St. Benedict wistfully says in his Holy Rule for Monks. Even one hundred and fifty a week create indigestion if they are served together. The rather athletic concept of desert sanctity was admirable, but hardly fits the sensitive or unsensitive cleric of our day. Some psalms are didactic or historical poems: they should be read as such in their own good time as Scripture lessons. Others carry a seasonal flavor and should be used in their season only: 117 for Easter, 50 for Passiontide, 71 for Epiphany, 84, 79, and 21 for Advent, 67 for Pentecost, 44 for feasts of Our Lady and Dedication. Some used at Mass (*Iudica, Lavabo*), others at Baptism, at weddings, and funerals. If these psalms are used at their seasonal time or sacred occasion, if the historical psalms are read, not recited, there will be ample psalms that would make up the body—one psalm per canonical hour of any description—of the psalter of the Church in her clerics' daily Office.

Instead of cramming three Psalm graduales into the slim body of one of the "little hours," which makes the savoring of them almost impossible, there would be one psalm, changing from day to day. There is no choir for the pastoral clergy and the missionary. The breviary long ago assumed the character of a great prayer book. It should have become then the source from which springs the fervent, devotional life of the cleric above all, and it should have formed and inspired his vocabulary in his homilies and sermons, in the confessional, and beside the sick bed. The psalms, if wisely selected, not measured by inches and verses, would not need labored allegories to string them together. They seem to be without an individual eschatology; they never seem to be aware of a hereafter: all is present, present misery or triumph, rescue and survival. Thus they represent an earlier stage of Judaism, that either leads to an attitude which skips over the gravest facts of our faith or needs all the amplification of Christian hymnody and the Fathers' and Doctors' counterweight. One more reason to go easy on the numbers and to space them safely within the frame of Christian ethics, eschatology, and Soteriology.

I have not changed my mind: I would say that the breviary should be in the spoken language of our time. We are not losing the bond of unity or its expression; it is not the Latin sound that keeps us in one fold; it is—outside of grace—the common heritage of thoughts and emotions that exist only when expressed with understanding.

To sum up: vernacular—yes; revision of the Scripture reading and its amplification and better distribution—yes; reduction of the day hours according to the rhythm of pastoral life—yes; preservation of the best hymns, antiphons and responsories—yes; a calendar centering with emphasis on the Redeemer and His work, reduction of the sanctoral part—yes; weeding out of psalms, assigning them to their functional places in rites and seasons on the one hand, and moving the less apt ones for prayer to the lesson part of the breviary, if they are didactic or mere historical poems—yes; to give the Divine Office more than a token preference over the "real prayer," to make it, by changing it from monastic to pastoral inspiration, the foremost means toward prayer of contemplation—emphatically, yes. The existing dualism of "official duty prayers" to be performed for obedience's sake, but without spiritual nourishment, except *per accident* (via obedience) and those prayers that seem to give per se—a rather slim diet, compared with the unused resources of the performance prayer—the nourishment of prayer—this dualism should be overcome. I for one trust that it can be overcome by a reform without destroying all that tradition has bequeathed to us, more than the present untapped riches ever can.

It seems appropriate to discuss here the problem of the psalter of Pius XII that was made by Cardinal Bea and his staff at the Pontifical Biblical Institute in Rome. Gregorian musicologists, first-rate experts of the late Latin, as it was developed by the Fathers and the Church at the time of Pope Damasus I and St. Jerome have protested that the psalter is unsuitable for Gregorian chant and is an academic Latin of pseudo-ciceronian hue and vocabulary. In angry tones the translators are asked, why the completely Latinized and lovely word *jubilate* had to make room for the colorless "celebrate" or its equivalents, to quote but one example in a hundred. All I have read against the new psalter has its value, and it seems that a sort of high-school Latin has taken the place of a language organically wedded to tradition. But that is not the question at all.

The question really: Does the new psalter come closer to the original Hebrew text? Is it a better base for translation into the vernacular? This is a concern for the liturgy, and we do not mention the importance of a correct text for dogma and kerygma. Why should a protagonist of the vernacular be involved in the merits of style, rhythm, and musical qualities of a standard basic text to be used for professional dogmatic, moral, canonistic, kerygmatic discussions and for translation? What he should be concerned about is an English version of the corrected text and the poetic and stylistic value of this version. In the meantime, since there are no great prose and verse writers around, why not use a corrected King James Version? Its "heretical and schismatic" authors did a superb job, I am told: do we screen every contractor and bricklayer, designer and electrician for orthodoxy and moral acceptability when we build churches and supply them with furnishings and sacred vessels? Continental Catholics have accepted hymns from other sources by the carload; is our squeamishness caused by pride, pique, and righteousness or by the fear of indifferentism? I was vastly amused when I heard a Presbyterian congregation sing "Faith of Our Fathers," which I have heard in Catholic gatherings, sometimes militantly

Catholic demonstrations. The translators may have been wrong, deadly so, but they certainly provided the English-speaking peoples with a fine and prayerful text, which needs only a few amendments to suit our breviary, while none of the earlier or later attempts, including Knox, have the qualities of this version. But esthetic arguments are not paramount. It is the correctness and the easy flow of the text that make it usable for our breviary: for this the Pian Psalter furnishes the base.

The breviary reform is on its way. A commission of experts is dealing with it, duly appointed by him who has the power exclusively to do so: the Sovereign Pontiff. Therefore these remarks are offered merely as the contribution. AD NUTUM PONTIFICIS.

8

Liturgy and Devotion

THE IMITATION OF CHRIST

There are those who like to present the Middle Ages as "golden," giving the impression that all was well until the Reformation upset the peaceful pattern of undisturbed faith. It would be more realistic—and more consoling to the present generation—if we realized how torn and restless the ages of faith actually were. But despite all the disturbing and sometimes sordid details of medieval history, we too come to the conclusion that it was an age in Western history deeply concerned with the image of God and restless in its effort to find Him.

Just before the simultaneous great disintegration of religious unity in the Reformation and the intellectual discoveries of the Renaissance, a religious revival took place among the earnest-minded and sincere-hearted people around the lower Rhine. It was a great movement of religious rebirth—sparked by laymen and supported by secular priests—known as the *Devotio Moderna,* the "Modern Devotion." It should be better known and more profoundly understood. The most famous of the men involved in this revival were Gerard Groote (born 1340), his successor Florence Radewijn (born 1350), and above all, Thomas Hemerken (born 1380), called "à Kempis" because he hailed from Kempen, a small town in the Rhenish plain not far from Cologne. Hemerken was the movement's greatest writer, although others who were its pupils, like the great Cardinal Nicholas of Cues, Erasmus of Rotterdam, and many prominent leaders on both sides of the Reformation, among them Ignatius Loyola and John Calvin, are its spiritual off-spring. The laymen were organized in a congregation called "The Brothers of the Common Life." The clerical members who followed the same principles in their renewed and "interiorized" spiritual lives gathered as the Canons of Windesheim, a small town near Zwolle, Holland. They in turn served as chaplains and spiritual directors in the houses and the excellent schools the Brothers soon established in the major cities of the lowlands and northern France.

It almost seems possible to say that all that is now recognized as being positive in the Reformation—its call for reform, its concern with the religion of the heart and conscience, its emphasis on in-teriorness and sincerity, its recourse to the Scriptures, its opposition to rote and dead formula in religious practice—was foreshadowed in this movement; when the catastrophe finally broke in 1517 it was only too easy for some of its members to mistake the Reformers for God-sent prophets; many of them followed them out of the Church, misled by what was negative in the Reformation—its open rebellion, its defiance of authority, and its elevation of the individual to a position where he took supreme command over his spiritual affairs in the name of conscience. Although these elements were absent from the *Devotio Moderna,* they were foreshadowed in its contempt for the intellectual approach to the Faith, for theological speculation and dogmatic preciseness summarized in sharply chiseled formulas and definitions. When Thomas Hemerken writes that it is "better to feel compunction than to know the accurate definition of it," and when he does this in a context that conveys the general impression that this is more than an obvious truth, it becomes evident that it is an attitude and a pattern of a subtle anti-intellectualism hovering over an age surfeited with a decaying, late, and inferior scholasticism. Not only was there a general cry for reform of the Church "in head and limbs," but there was also a groan for relief from the verbaliz-ings of the later schoolmen who were no equals of Thomas Aquinas, Bonaventure, and Duns Scotus. In other words, their cry for the religion of the heart and for the word of God without philosophy was a sound and genuine reaction to a good thing overdone. And like all reactions, it went so far in the opposite direction as to become dangerous.

This danger became visible to the naked eye in the Reformation, when Luther called reason a harlot. No one among the followers of the *Devotio Moderna*, especially not their greatest writer Thomas Hemerken, ever went so far, but the trend was there, and with it piety became no longer communal but almost purely individual. There is also in the *Devotio Moderna* a late medieval preoccupation with the nearly exclusive identification of Christ's Redemption with His suffering, and little of His victory and triumph. It is a very "moral," an almost sour and slightly joyless version of the Good Tidings, apparent visually in the paintings of the Flemish primitives and their North German counterparts who worked with an exclusive interest in the Passion, especially in its physical aspects.

This summary is necessary to give our book, *The Imitation of Christ*, its background. It is a classic, and it rivals the Bible itself in numbers of editions and reprints. It has served such great saints as Ignatius and others. Its prestige is such that one is tempted to lift it out of its historical background and to regard it as absolute, since it is so timeless and needs no further commendation. However, if the Old Testament has to be focused by the New, and the New in its turn, by the living tradition of the Church and by the light thrown upon it by research, this book cannot be declared above an evaluation. It will always remain one of the great books of mankind, not alone for Catholics, but for all others who strive after the imitation of Christ, using it for their own ascent to God.

The Imitation of Christ was written by Thomas Hemerken, in spite of all the learned attempts to give one of his brethren the credit for it. It is a true product of the *Devotio Moderna*, even in its form, because it is written in pithy aphorisms with utter disregard for system and logical order. Not that there is anything not logical in it, but its clear thoughts and reasonable progressions avoid a visible and preconceived shape, as you would find it in a textbook or a *Summa Theologica*. You could, with the exception of the fourth book, which deals with the Eucharist in its late medieval form of piety (which form largely, thanks to this very treatment, is still ours), rearrange its chapters or books and even the aphorisms within the chapters without suffering much harm, so loosely is it strung together. And mind you, this is no serious shortcoming: it wants to lead to prayer and it does. It wants to bridge the gap between the two halves of Christian life, worship and doing, and it does. It wants to impress on the reader a religion of the heart and the conscience, as against an outward and busy performance consisting in formalities and near superstitious and miracle-hungry claptrap, and it succeeds. Its devotion is based on scriptural sayings and endeavors to distill out of the Gospels a rule of earnest, devout and godly life, which it does without fail.

Thomas Hemerken in his manly piety is opposed to all flamboyant gestures. He loathes frills and lacework and leads the reader directly to the center of his faith: Christ Who assumes suffering and death, and our task is to follow Him in this. Hemerken does this without pampering us, without sugaring the sometimes bitter truth, without cushioning the hard impact of the cross Christ lays on the shoulders of all men. He talks like a good confessor of the old school, but like one who knows man's heart, not with psychoanalytically trained insight, but with an instinct for human deviousness, frailty and self-deception. He is not a Jansenist, or full of gloom, but he is matter of fact and earnest. Nobody can run away from death nor from the cross of his life: let us face it and go on our way with honesty and courage. Yet a Dominican may object to the lack of speculative system and of organization in Thomas Hemerken's masterpiece; a Franciscan might find it a bit cheerless and dour; a Benedictine would miss the expansiveness that goes with community life and the liturgy as a continuation of the table round of the Last Supper; a Jesuit will look in vain for greater emphasis on the apostolic aspect of complete Christianity; the little regard the author seems to display for the mystical stages may astonish the Carmelite; the layman will search high and low for a positive word on married love and the family; the priest of our day will miss any reference on the social implications of the Gospel and the duty of the Christian to permeate the economic and political system with the oil of Christ. Yet all of them will use this great book and be richer therefor. It will fill all of them with a consciousness of one aspect of true sanctity: a single-minded and—shall we say—direct contempt of all that is mediate and of no lasting consequence for our salvation.

The Imitation of Christ, which was translated into English as early as the sixteenth century by Richard Whitford, a friend of St. Thomas More, in the virile and "earth-near" English of his day, and again in the pithy English of the eighteenth century by Bishop Challoner, has been translated many times since in a competitive effort to render it in the full richness of its Latin original.

Those who have used this great stirrer of souls and admonisher of hearts have their preferences, but some chapters, like the ones on the "Royal Road of the Cross" (Book I, Chapter 12), "On the Consideration of Oneself" (II, 5), the "Proof of a True Lover" (III, 6), on "True Comfort in God Alone" (III, 15), on "The Four Things That Bring Much Peace" (III, 23), "On Self-Love," "Inconstancy of the Human Heart" and a few more: these are beyond doubt favorites of all who use this book as a guide to meditation.

"Why doest thou then dread," Hemerken writes in Book II, Chapter 12, "to take upon thyself the cross: it is the very way to the Kingdom of Heaven and there is none other. In the cross is health and life and defence from our enemy; it puts into us heavenly sweetness; it gives our mind strength, our spirit joy, exalted virtue, full perfection of holiness: there is no health of soul nor hope of everlasting life, but through the power of the cross. . . . Go where thou wilt and seek what thou wouldst; never shalt thou find, above thee or beneath thee, within thee or without thee . . . a more sure way to Christ than the way of the Holy Cross. Dispose all things after thy own will and yet thou shalt find that thou needs must suffer somewhat, either with thy will or against thy will. And thus thou shalt always find the cross: sometimes thou feelest forsaken by God, sometimes vexed by thy neighbor and, what is even worse pain, thou wilt be a burden to thyself. There is no deliverance but to suffer till it please almighty God in His goodness otherwise to dispose for thee. It is He who desireth thou shalt learn to suffer with consolation and wholly to submit to Him to be made meeker by tribulation than thou werest before."

This seems to be "a hard speech" to our present fainthearted and soft generation, according to our own interpretation of faith. But Thomas Hemerken has a grave and firm quality in his writing that will stand the test of life. There is no denying that he sounds desperately like Jesus Himself, and that while reading and reluctantly admitting the truth of his stern sayings, we modern Christians experience the embarrassing feeling that we stand on the side of Sadducees and Pharisees: either we try hard to explain away the cross or we replace it with narrow and meticulous observances, like the pilgrimages and the desire for sure-fire and sensational devotions that Thomas scorns so eloquently. All of these are but escapes from reality into patterns cunningly designed by human cowardice. Thomas Hemerken's writing is full of such wisdom close to the Gospel. Although we might find him to be the child of his era, the gist of his message is as timeless and direct as his Master's, which also speaks of a "soft and adulterous generation." In an age where the pursuit of happiness is taken to mean hedonism, the craving of pleasure, the clear sound of this trumpet voice from the Mount of the Sermon and from Calvary is as salutary now as it was in his own day, when laymen shamed the guardians of the Gospel by their initiative in the *Devotio Moderna.*

Even his severest critics have to admit one thing: that Thomas Hemerken built his appeal to man on Christ as the center. He shuns all sweetness outside the Savior's, and takes Him as person alive and real. There is no softening or cushioning or dilution of the Word. He is on guard, without expressly saying so, against the coming great relapse into a perverted stage of an Old Testament phase of religion—of "faith" as a means of success and of painless living without risk, of "faith" that is no more daring than safety devices and insurance policies. Though we miss in Thomas Hemerken some of

Christianity's more joyful aspects, and although he sounds at times more stoic than Christian, there is a quality in him that shatters all vanity, a manliness that shuns softness and a simplicity that lays bare the devious ruses of our hearts: Thomas à Kempis should be read by our generation to purify it from the subtle secularism that is enveloping the devout almost as much as the worldly.

SPIRITUAL GROWTH: A PROGRESSIVE SHARING OF DIVINE NATURE
(2 Peter 1:4)

Through created grace the uncreated source of sanctification, the Third Person in the Trinity of Father and Son and Holy Spirit, makes real what the words of St. Peter so starkly propose. It is a fact that has to be believed by supernatural faith. It transcends our natural powers of cognition. Few are privileged to have an experience that clearly and undisputedly raises them to that altitude which St. Paul calls *tritos ouranos,* the third heaven. He is unable to put the experience into human words, nor can he himself distinguish whether his body shared this experience or not. It was an experience of more sublime character than such states as the imprinting of stigmata, or the mystical phenomena that the world finds so fascinating, which the true mystics like St. John of the Cross regard as initial stages to be transcended.

No man among us common mortals who live, or hope to live, by faith know by experience, if this state has anything in common with the beatific vision. The witnesses indicate that it is a mere foretaste of what no eye has seen, nor ear heard, nor of what has come into the heart of man, but has been prepared for them that love Him. This *koinonia,* this "having or holding in common with" God His very nature (Preface for the Feast of the Ascension) is proclaimed the goal of the Incarnation: "Who in full sight of the Apostles was raised into heaven to give that we might be sharers of His Divinity." This is the "theandric" condition of the redeemed. By Baptism all

are introduced into this divine life. This is therefore the basic fact
that constitutes the Catholic "way" of sanctification.

All sacramental life is in *genere signi*, built on reality-carrying
symbolism. The Church uses the most vital language that equals in
its realism the Canticle of Solomon. For instance in the Great Night
at the Blessing of the Font: "Make fertile this water, readied to beget
men anew by the hidden (*arcana*) commingling of His Divinity
(*numen*), that, after conceiving sanctification, from the stainless
womb of the divine spring, reborn into a new creation, a heavenly
offspring may emerge . . . that Grace as Mother (*mater gratia*)
may bear all into one childhood" (*infantia* here carrying the overtones of dependency, muteness in the face of God's holy Father-
hood). There is also the emphatic "*una,*" the oneness into which are
all to be born. When this Preface was sung for the first time, perhaps in Leo's day around A.D. 400 or before, this *koinonia* was
obviously very much alive in the mind of its composer.

It seems, at least on a corporate level, that Peter's statement:
"sharing divine nature," was borne out by practical faith at one time
in the Church; the things about which the Preface "hymns and
sings" are real on the level of faith, but nobody claimed that they
also must be experienced to be real. Is there then, apart from the
symbolic, sacramental life that normally does not include a conscious and "felt" awareness comparable to a mystic experience, an
unrelated and independent mystic life, properly so called? Does
liturgical prayer as opposed to sacramental union grow on different
branches of the common tree?

This is a burning problem. Many religious have asked this question in one form or another. We attend at daily Mass, receive daily
Communion and share in other parts of the liturgy, like the solemn
praise of God in our Office in common or in private. Since these
exercises are prescribed by law, we have a tendency to regard them
as a burden patiently borne in filial obedience. Yet in our hearts we
think of mental prayer as the prayer that really mobilizes our inte-
rior forces. For centuries we now have had systems and methods for
this prayer. A few reach the state of acquired or of infused contempla-

tion to which Holy Communion as well as a Rosary may be the springboard. This has been held up before a large public as the promised land of monks and nuns, nay, of devout people in the world.

A well known writer in this field once complained about the condition he had observed: that the breviary seemed to mean nothing to those who strove after contemplation. It was unrelated to the true spiritual life and really a form of mortification via unquestioning obedience. The late Dom Anselm Stolz has taken care of this problem in a classical monograph and shown that true contemplation in the religion of Incarnation and of the sacraments is essentially a fruit of this sacramental life. By its character and its explicit form the Office is, however, part and parcel of the sacramental system of the Church, an outgrowth of the Holy Eucharist, and a continuation of the Mass through the day.

Nor is justice done either to the contemplative life or to the sacramento-liturgical life if we resort to the well known method of using bits and snatches of Scripture selected by momentary intuition as *Points d'Appui* to kick ourselves off or to be raised into a soaring position of contemplation. This method is, of course, neither bad nor forbidden, but that is not the question: it would remain accidental to the liturgy and not be an answer to the problem how to integrate practical symbolism into the road on which we safely travel to God the Unknown and Unseen. God forbid that we should suggest that such use of the liturgy were illicit: we envy the person who journeys thus light-footedly through earthly life, while the rest of us plod along on the low road. It would be strange, if the religion which is founded on the Incarnation and which seems to live by sacraments regarded these basic things as destined for those who are as yet *psychikoi*, dull and fleshly, while the *pneumatikoi*, the enlightened and spiritual, use the more excellent way of St. Paul's. It would be as if the two lives ran parallel, never meeting but in the Infinite. The sacraments would then become a device that serves the less spiritual, because they needed *visibilia*, while the more spiritual are already swept forward toward the *invisibilia* and only by humility and charity submit to the ways of the common folk, as Christ submitted to John's baptism. In this fashion of thinking the liturgy would become an exercise of humility, a condescending to the level of the multitude. And what does this make of the Incarnation and Crucifixion, if we follow the thought to its logical conclusions? Does there not lurk behind this mentality a faint tendency toward crypto-Platonism? A mild contempt for the things of the senses, however concealed it is, may be the beginning of Manicheism.

In the commonly practiced method the liturgy provides a kind of peg to which one can latch one's prayer, few and far between in the flow of sacred texts. A word, a phrase, an image or a tune provides a platform for a higher plane where one's spirit soars above sound and print. Of course there is a way of rationalizing. We take refuge in the "Church": *she* prays and praises in unending hymns the heavenly Bridegroom, and for this praise our voices provide the equipment. The meaning of the breviary texts is however Eucharistic in the sense that it spreads the foremass and the proper of the day and season over the day in regular intervals in order to incorporate our whole life into the glory and praise rendered by us in the only acceptable sacrifice of the New Covenant. Considerations like these and a general intention of "doing what the Church does" may raise us above the distaste and the feeling of dissatisfaction which otherwise possesses us all too easily. What we hear and read remains largely unrealized and unfulfilled as far as our own heart and mind are concerned, but the "Church" makes up for it: again the fruit of this performance is borne by obedience and sacrifice of the will, rather than by the liturgy itself. The breviary should therefore be kept next to the hair shirt and the discipline.

This attitude has afflicted even the Mass itself, so that a sort of "angelism" has infected our participation: only the consecration counts, the Real Presence and the "Meeting" of Holy Communion; the rest is in this method a negligible addition, man-made and not even instrumental any longer. Like pure spirits in the presence of the Infinite, to speak according to our weak analogical powers, such an attitude essays to seize God without intermediary.

It is also possible to see why the kind of dogmatic theology which is inspired by the controversies of the last few hundred years is not helpful in establishing a sounder relationship between the subject, the sign of the sacrament, and the object of its signification.

To exemplify what we mean, let us examine the Holy Eucharist. Where our spiritual writers, our everyday and popularized literature and preaching stand, is familiar to all observers. The sacramental signs, the species and symbolism, are boldly ignored and we rush into what are supposed to be the realities, minus the species. What was meant to be a *foreshadowing* of the heavenly banquet, a communal feasting of the redeemed, becomes an *anticipation* of heaven almost without the brethren. One thought can show us what has happened: What would we do, if tomorrow the Vicar of Christ decreed that instead of the thin wafer, a bulky piece of leavened bread were to be used, and besides, the Cup of the Sacred Blood were reintroduced for the Communion of all? What would be done to our spirituality, if together with this the words of the consecration had to be chanted again in a tongue that all understood? If we took up again the solemn breaking of the Bread for Communion, the reception of our consecrated morsel on "the throne of our hand," and if all of us sang psalms while receiving the Sacred Food? I am neither advocating such a return to archaic and long-forgotten forms, nor am I predicting that the Holy See will ever do even only part of this. In this context it is used only to illustrate how far we have gone in disembodying the liturgy first in adapting the outward things and prior to this in pinpointing *selected* truths and in letting other truths wither away in practice and making them too pale in theory. We should not forget that the martyrs and Fathers had a Mass that was closer in outward appearance to the Supper of the Lord and was called the "Breaking of the Bread." Would it not be risky to maintain that our present condition is all progress and a purification of what Christ instituted?

Some theologian may maintain that these changes were wrought to a greater "spiritualizing" of the things that Christ saw fit to give a less sophisticated humanity. Controversy, pastoral convenience, and an overlapping of individual mysticism into liturgical territory may have been the real causes for the changes. A retrenching and reorientation have to take place before we can hope to be able to take the *species liturgica* as a means of apprehending grace in its full signification and not as a mere container pouring forth grace. Without outward changes and with full acceptance of the present forms, we must yet try to integrate our spiritual lives into the world of signs and symbols of the sacraments, especially the Eucharist, or we shall forever be condemned to the state of mind which is bent on wearing the liturgy as a hair shirt instead of as "eyeglasses" to see better and to correct our spiritual sight. Like all comparisons and parables, this one limps and should not be pressed.

We must adjust ourselves to seeing the signs as signifiers, as symbols, adequate symbols, of the signified realities they contain. Their meaning carries over into all its details without lapsing into a purely naturalistic interpretation of the symbols. That would be the pitfall this side of the species, while the other, excessive spiritualization, has been mentioned above. We need not be conscious of the problem at all times, because it would rob us of the simplicity that is required of unreflected and genuine life. Let the Incarnation be our guide to the sacraments, and we are on safe ground. St. Leo the Great gave us the clear statement that "what was visible in Christ, is now gone into the sacraments." Therefore the liturgical attitude is the one that assumes the posture of one who sees and hears Christ, when the liturgy is concerned.

From these remarks it is obvious that it is through our incorporation in Christ's Body, the Church, that we share Divine nature, more precisely through created grace effected by the Holy Spirit. For reasons of convenience the normal rite of incorporation is Baptism by infusion. Yet, the *Rituale Romanum* still assumes as first choice that of immersion. Concerning ourselves with cause and effect and essential requirements, infusion is all we need. But from the viewpoint of full signification the immersion rite yields more results, as it goes beyond the mere ablution and brings out the two biblical aspects of rebirth out of the maternal womb of the Church (so amply referred to in the benediction of the font) and of burial and resurrection. The ritual conformation of the member to the Head has a reality all its own which is sacramental and must go beyond mere intentional signification or illustration. The full liturgy of Baptism is steeped in the Death-Redemption of Christ according to the teaching of St. Paul and the promise of Our Lord to Nicodemus.

Nor are the words of the consecration of the Sacred Chrism mere poetic flourishes. We need not accept Denys the Areopagite's doctrine which sees a real presence of the Holy Spirit in Chrism after its consecration, but there still remain the earnest statements that this sacred oil, when applied to a baptized Christian confirms and enlarges the indelible character by giving the *Miles Christi* four potentialities: of priesthood, of martyrdom, of kingship and prophetdom, perfecting the baptismal character into adult and mature membership in Christ. Baptism is sonship of God, Confirmation assimilates us *in potentia* to the maturity of Christ and responsibility for His Mystical Body. Our task from then on is the actualizing of these seminal "components" of our baptismal character which ordains us to a certain degree into the sharing of Christ's redemptive and sacerdotal role. We have the grace; we then must raise our nature to an adequation of these gifts which are not only the four components, but also the seven gifts enumerated in the rite of "perfecting and confirming Baptism" by its complementary sacrament.

The liturgy of these two sacraments unfolds fuller riches than the average Christian suspects: Baptism in its bare aspect as a washing away of sins and a clothing with the unspotted garment of sanctifying grace (which is the sum of ideas available to the average catechism-trained layman) lacks what might be called the *organic* character of the full sacrament with all its implications and overtones. So also is Confirmation boldly summarized by the words: "we become soldiers in Christ's army." This, truly, is not so full and organic in content as it will be if we see it in its liturgical plenitude when the whole rite of both the consecration of chrism and confirmation is contemplated. Human concepts, even the most theological ones, are analogical and insufficient to grasp the reality for which we grope in man's language and in his systematic efforts with the help of tools forged by philosophy. It should by now already be clear that the liturgy applied to the two basic sacraments yields a wealth of vital and almost "umbilical" cords carrying floods of supernatural "sap" to the very gates of our souls, which can be unlocked by the key of an intelligent grasp of the liturgy. All this is contained in the reality of the sacramental world. The conceptual wealth, clothed in images, is only an analogy of the reality apprehended by faith "that seeks understanding."

When we come to a discussion of the Eucharist, the stream of concepts and the volume of overtone swells to even greater volume. Not only must we reflect on the signs of bread and wine and sacred words, more than the "cause-effect" posture of lesser and minor scholastic epigones, but we have this principle of growth by Christ imbedded in a great many auxiliary devices.

First there is more than the bare Consecration and Communion: we have the whole Mass, making the presence of Christ particularized and individualized. One of the greatest and most consequential events in liturgical history was the linking together of the synagogal service, the foremass (with its satellites scattered in the space of the Eucharist proper, Offertory, Secret, Preface, Communion antiphon-and-psalm, and Postcommunion) and the sacrificial banquet, the fusing of the Word and of the verbal Presence of Christ with the sacramental Presence into one liturgical unit. This has engendered participations of the most fertile and vital kind. The intentional and immediate Presence in the Gospel, then through a medium in the Epistle, in the responsories, antiphons, psalms and hymns, make the Consecration and Communion assume a definite hue gently imprinting an image of great reality on the celebrating Church and her members. In the technical language of the theologians the words of Scripture are sacramentals. In the liturgy they must be seen as part and parcel of the Holy Eucharist through which the celebrating Church—and it is important to remember that the individual participates as at a banquet, as a member of the Church—*realizes herself* as the Christ in a *particular* realization spotlighted out of the whole "work of Redemption" for this very occasion.

Second: what is thus particularized and made palatable in selective and sectional slices is assembled to a totality by the temporal cycles of the year. The principle of motion is here not a historical repristination, an abridged sort of life of Christ in Sunday lessons or of dramatized biblical history. It is the projection of the life of the Church, a yearly cycle of her pilgrimage and growth through time into eternity. Starting with Septuagesima Sunday the liturgical year opens with the spring rites: we prepare for the new Life through Resurrection. The access to it is arduous and requires that we go through mortification, passion, and death: here again Christ is present every day in the twofold manner of the Mass. From Pasch to fall Christ teaches us in liturgy in the feastday and Sunday Masses and consolidates the annual rebirth of the paschal night in the liturgy of the time. From the fall Ember days and the eighteenth Sunday after Pentecost until Candlemas and the last Sunday after the Epiphany, gradually gaining intensity of thought and mood, the parousia-Advent, the Teleiosis, is the goal. The spiritual gaze is toward eternity and the future. In well-measured intervals, with time given for all the Presences (*parousiai*) to be better assimilated into the spiritual progress, we travel through these cycles annually, deeper rooted in Christ as our eternal contemporary: sacramentally and liturgically we are contemporary with the Master and Lord and His "Opus Redemptionis."

Third: the liturgy has its "feeders" funneling the Mass-presence over the whole day in the day hours of the Office. Like sound waves of the Mass echoing through day and night these services bring to the divisions of the day—night, sunrise, the beginning of work, midmorning, noon, midafternoon, sunset and retiring hour—the Christ of the Mass, a facet of the whole Christ as we live Him during the year's cycles. These cyles are again moved forward by our own life cycles and those of the Church in her history. The liturgy is therefore in a spiritual way to be compared with the atomic universe from the nucleus of the atom circled by its satellites to the rotating worlds of the immense galaxies.

This is not to be understood as a guide for chosen individuals for their lonely journey through life, because the sacramental life of the Church not only involves an official minister of the sacraments and visible signs, but the Church itself which is the baptized brethren assembled. It does not mean that liturgical piety is not immensely personal. Our rites are so protective of the dignity of the individual and so chaste in emotion and gesture that degrees of intimate union are hidden from the prying eye of the *mysts* of the great mystery of the Church. The balance between the alert and the dull, the morally weak and the strong, the earthly minded and the spiritually sensitive, the simple and the sophisticated is marvelously established by the liturgy in which each man can be at home and find Jesus Christ and through Him the Father. That the liturgy is the ordinary way does not mean that it is geared to the lowest common denominator and addresses itself to the senses only, leaving the mystic to dig himself his own cisterns in greater depth. It is a liturgical text that speaks of the *sobria ebrietas: "Laeti bibamus sobriam ebrietatem Spiritus":* Let us drink with joy the sober drunkenness of the Spirit.

The more man seeks light in his faith, the more he realizes that God remains Mystery and the Unknown. Father Victor White, O.P., in his great book *God the Unknown* quotes the prince of the Scholastics, St. Thomas Aquinas: "We are most perfectly at one with Him when we know that He is utterly unknown," or as he states himself: "We are most in His light when we are most in the dark about Him." *Multifariam Multisque modis* has God spoken to us, till at last He spoke His Word made *flesh.* What was visible in Christ is now in His sacraments. As long as we live in this flesh, He is our sole Mediator through whom we apprehend the Mystery of Mysteries.

Index